For my real *family*

Contents

Foreword, My Ass—This Is a Contract

by Denis Hamill

When a guy named Goumba asks you to write a "foreword," you take a step backwards and throw up your hands. If his last name is Sialiano, you get to live and laugh about it. But he gives you a contract: "I need for you to write up a foreword for my book, *So You Wanna Be a Mobster.*"

"Done, Goumba," I sez.

"I need it by Friday—*a capi?*" he says. On Thursday.

Nice.

"Goumba Johnny" Sialiano has been making me laugh for about ten years now, ever since my then-teenage daughters Katie and Nell, of Bay Ridge, Brooklyn—where a lot of the corpses in this book were found in trunks of Cadillacs with Goumba's KTU radio show still playing on the car radio—first asked me to listen. Didn't matter if the music he played sounded like the last plane crash I covered for the *Daily News.* Goumba Johnny made you piss your drawers in the morning before you made it to the john. His "Ballbuster" and "War of the Roses" routines, nailing unsuspecting listeners live on the air, became radio classics.

So I made it my business to meet and write about Goumba Johnny—this screwball with the movie-star looks and the body by Rikers, out of the Bronx—who made a whole city laugh itself awake every morning. You don't find too many guys who can make teenage girls and their jaded father howl at the same wicked jokes and merciless routines. "This is my kind of button man," I said. "He doesn't just get laughs—he kills."

Then Goumba had to go and spoil it all by revealing a wimpy Runyonesque human side. Here was a guy name of Goumba who, it turns out, supported more charities than Mother Teresa, taking time out of his personal life to raise money for cancer, kidney disease, leukemia, autism, and child abuse.

One treacherous December morning, a perfect day for a cold-blooded Yuletide hit, here was Goumba Johnny all the way out in the ass end of Sheepshead Bay, Brooklyn, at Pips Comedy Club, broadcasting a live remote and having citizens drop off checks and toys for Toys for Tots for the Tiny Tims of the city whose only toys would be the ones he forwarded to them from his listeners. Goumba caused a traffic jam on Emmons Avenue as fans flocked with money and gifts, looking to meet the wacko who sent them to work slap-happy every morning.

Humbug, I thought. I want ballbusting, shiv-in-the-belly-laughs, and endless dark jokes in the grim morning. Instead, here was Goumba putting his big mouth where his money was in front of a microphone, shaking down bad-ass Brooklyn for the kids who had been dealt a bad hand from a stacked deck in life.

In between charity spiels, Goumba spared no ethnic group his stiletto. The Irish, Jews, Blacks, Hispanics, gays, all got sliced up into calamari. But he saved the kill for his own tribe, unloading a lifetime of observations about Italian mothers, grandmothers, wannabes, and wiseguys—all of it done in pure self-effacing fun.

I've done several stories on Goumba since, and almost all of them had to do with some new charity he was promoting. I've seen him perform stand-up live on the upscale stages of the best comedy venues in Manhattan and billion-dollar casino hotels in Atlantic City, and I've seen him at fundraisers for Cooley's anemia in gymnasiums in Staten Island, Jersey, and Queens. A couple of years ago, when Tony "Paulie Walnuts" Sirico gathered the entire cast of *The Sopranos* to a fundraiser at a Gatsbyesque estate in Long Island, he assigned the emcee contract to the only man in America who could pull the trigger. Goumba grabbed the mic, busted balls, told jokes, had the audience in stitches, and ran the raffles. Within two hours he'd raised close to a half-million bucks for St. Jude's Hospital for kids with cancer. By night's end he had grown mooks with no necks and bent noses reduced to tears when he introduced some of the sick kids who would now get a second shot at life.

But fear not: The next morning Goumba was back on the air, tearing his listeners new laugh holes with his fierce on-air antics. That's what you'll find in these pages: A cold-blooded laugh assassin with a heart of gold . . . that just fell off the back of a truck.

Leave the cannolis, take the book.

Goumba Speaks

Why I'm the Perfect Guy
to Write This Book

I WAS BORN AND RAISED ON THE MEAN STREETS OF THE BRONX, NEW York City. Just about everyone I knew and hung out with was associated, one way or the other, with the mob. The Bronx and Yonkers was lousy with wiseguys when I was a kid.

It may sound like a cliché now, but back then you could always tell a mobster or a wiseguy when one of them passed you on the sidewalk. For one thing, they always radiated an air of danger. For another, they always had big wads of cash, flashy clothes, and brand-new Caddies. And they always seemed to have names like Joey the Hammer, Bobby Meatballs, Frankie the Animal, and Pete the Dentist. (So called because he had a very effective way of persuading delinquent loan-shark cus-tomers to pay off—he'd yank their teeth out with needle-nose pliers. And without the benefit of Novocain.)

Growing up in the Bronx, most of my friends' dads were in the life. Mickey Z's father, for example, was a juice man (col-lector of extortion payments) for the Genovese mob. Tommy C's father ran a bookie joint on East Tremont Avenue for the Lucchese family. Joey D's dad was in cement—literally, after he was caught skimming money from the Bricklayers Local. Legend has it that he's now supporting the foundation of a Third Avenue high-rise.

It all seemed normal, half the neighborhood being mobbed

up, because I didn't know any other way of life. So I know a little about the mob and wiseguys and the way they act and eat and dress and what motivates them (money, as a rule). What attracts outsiders (or "civilians") to the mob, in addition to the money and the broads, is the power that goes along with being part of something very big and very deadly. Think of the jerkoff who shoved your head into the boys' room toilet and flushed it, back in fifth grade. Wouldn't it be awesome to track him down on Classmates.com and pay him a visit with a couple of gorillas with names like Momo and Bobby the Basher? The local dry cleaner loses your favorite suit and is acting like an asshole about it? No problem—send Vinny Chunkhead and his magic cattle prod to deal with it. Your neighbor's poodle is pissing on your front lawn? Fugged-abouddit—just think of the expression on your neighbor's face when he wakes up with little Fifi's head on the pillow next to him.

I didn't become a wiseguy myself because it was very obvious that to get anywhere in these organizations, you'd be put in a position to kill or be killed. Not a good job for a kid who cried when his dog died. After that, you're on call 24/7 to carry out hits when your capo calls on you.

So now I'm writing about mob life instead of actually living it. Which I think in the long run is for the best, considering most of the guys I grew up with who went into "the life" are either dead or in the can.

That said, mob life can be rewarding. The trick is not to get killed or jailed.

Enjoy. And when dining in a five-star restaurant, always sit with your back to the wall, facing the front door. That way, you can duck under the table or out the back door when someone comes in blasting away. *Capisce?*

Introduction

Self-Help, Sicilian Style or, Get Ready to Help Yourself to Other People's Wealth and Property!

In this country, you gotta make the money first.
Then when you get the money, you get the power.
Then when you get the power, then you get the
women.

—Tony Montana (Al Pacino), *Scarface* (1983)

Do you dream of . . .

- Making your own hours?
- Dining in fine restaurants for free?
- Having beautiful women at your beck and call?
- Taking out your aggression on anyone you please, with no fear of retribution?
- Motivating a gang of burly, brainless thugs to do your bidding?
- Exploiting the laws of the land for your own financial gain?
- Earning the respect you deserve—or even better, scaring people into doing what you want?

What if you could have all of this—and then some? What if you could be the most respected "businessman" on the block— in your neighborhood, your gated community, or your trailer park? Guess what? You can. All it takes is a little ingenuity, a lot of "muscle," and a conscience that can be easily silenced for greater reward.

Isn't it about time you started your own Mafia family? So what's holding you back?

Is it because, traditionally, mobsters hail from big cities, like New York, Chicago, Boston, or Philly? Or that a mobster has to be connected in some ways to other mobsters—or that they have to be Italian?

Forget about the old rules. They no longer apply. That went out with Sammy the Bull's smashing the Omertà (the sacred Mafia code of silence). It doesn't matter if you live in Oatmeal, Nebraska; Bunyanville, South Dakota; Frog Hollow, Virginia; or even Pig's Knuckle, Indiana. You can be that scary guy, hanging out at nightclubs, planning lucrative crimes, and smoking impossible-to-get Cuban cigars, with beautiful women draped all over you like Armani suits.

And you don't even have to be Italian! Of course, you should have a passion for pasta and pinkie rings . . . but we'll get into that later.

Getting your own Mafia family up and running and reaping rewards is easier than you think. All it takes is a little know-how—and a lot of crime. This book will tell you everything you need to know.

Think of *So You Wanna Be a Mobster?* as a career guide for career criminals—the ultimate how-to-succeed-in-illegitimate-business guide for people tired of being suckers.

In the first chapter, you'll get a quick introduction to the traditional Mafia, and you'll find a role model after which to fashion your new persona. In chapter 2, you'll learn the ins and outs of the typical mafioso lifestyle. By chapter 3, you'll be ready to dive right in, with a framework for organizing your crime family and getting your operation off the ground.

Chapter 4 shows you who's who in a crime family, and gives you tips on how to "staff" yours. You'll also get tips for managing your "employees," as well as get a breakdown of incentives and perks you can offer. Chapter 5 looks at some of the most important players of all: the women. Who do you marry? How many goomars are enough? And how do you keep these women in line?

In chapter 6, your eyes will be opened to illicit business opportunities there for the taking. True, the traditional mob families may have cornered the market on fish, garbage hauling, prostitution, and other rackets, but there are plenty more opportunities available that you may never have considered. We'll share what these are, and show you how to make them your own.

By chapter 7, you'll see how to keep your business interests growing and thriving. You'll roll up your sleeves (so as not to bloody your cuffs) and learn all about the "manure" of organized crime: Violence. Who gets whacked? Who does the actually whacking? How can you effectively dispose of a body in the age of *CSI*?

Chapter 8 shows you how to make friends in high places, and how to use these people to keep your ass out of jail and your rap sheet squeaky clean.

Finally, in chapter 9, you'll be able to pause, look over the empire you created, see how to keep it sustained, and take a deep breath. And if you're lucky, it won't be your last . . .

With this handy, any-stronzo-can-follow-it guide, you'll be savoring all the delights of the good life in no time!

Oh, and by the way, this is a parody. If I find out you actually tried to start your own Mafia family, I may just have to send over one of my special friends from the neighborhood to your neighborhood to break your legs.

Salud!

Acknowledgments

Thanks to editor Gary Goldstein, who dreamed up this book and made some pretty funny suggestions and contributions. Thanks also to all the others at Kensington Publishing Corp. for their efforts, especially jacket designer Kris Noble. Melissa Hamberg took a great jacket photograph. Also, thanks to agent David Katz for looking out for me, and to the Don Buchwald Agency.

Thank you, Vincent Piazza, who came to writing sessions and helped brainstorm ideas like a madman. Thanks also to Joseph Ligotti, a.k.a. the Guy From Boston, Andy Lombardozzi; Jeffrey Gurian, Bart Raffaele, and Jill Niccolini for agreeing to play parts in this book and generously providing photos

And a heartfelt thank-you to Francine LaSala for her tremendous effort, time, and patience—and most of all, passion that made this book start and finish.

Special thanks to my KTU family, and especially to my real family, Mom, Dad, Tom, Janice, and my wife, Danielle.

Crime is merely a left-handed form of human endeavor.
—W. R. Burnett, *The Asphalt Jungle* (novel)

Keep your friends close but your enemies closer.
—Michael Corleone (Al Pacino), *Godfather, Part II* (1974)

I'm gonna go get the papers, get the papers.
—Jimmy Two Times (Anthony Powers), *GoodFellas* (1990)

CHAPTER 1

Meet the Mafia

or,

How a Bunch of Sicilian and Jewish Underachievers Created a Multibillion-Dollar Criminal Empire

TOM HAGEN (Robert Duvall): It's an old Sicilian message. It means Luca Brasi sleeps with the fishes.

MICHAEL CORLEONE (Al Pacino): Well, he certainly drank like one!

—A scene you never saw from *The Godfather* (Part I)

EVEN THOUGH THERE ARE MORE OPPORTUNITIES NOW THAN EVER before for the average Joe to become an average "Joey Bananas," you can't just sit back and decide to join the Mafia. A certain amount of groundwork needs to be laid, and that starts with doing your research. It's the same as if you were going to head into a legitimate venture, although I have no idea why anyone would want to do that. But that's another story.

It is absolutely essential to your success as a bona fide mafioso to know as much as you can about who came before you—who kicked ass and rocked their city, and who fucked

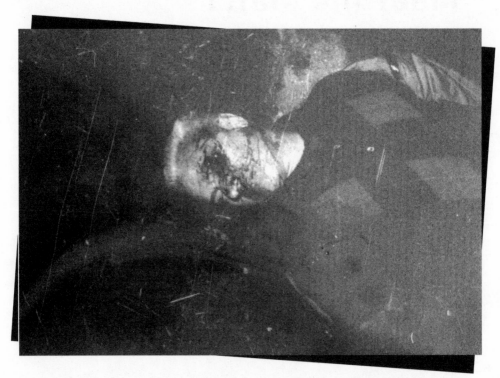

An eye for an eye: It's easy to get clipped in the Mafia, as this poor bastard found out the hard way. (photo courtesy U.S. Attorney's Office, Eastern District of New York)

up big time. (And in case you're too thick to grasp it yourself, the idea here is to model your Mafia career as closely as you can to those of the guys who didn't fuck up, because in gangland, "going out of business" is usually permanent. Remember, experience is the best teacher.

In this chapter, you will:

- Learn how and why the Mafia was born
- Learn about the baddest, meanest wiseguys who ever sported silk suits and pinkie rings, and follow the path to their success—or two bullets behind the ear
- Find your Mafia muse

What Started It?

Technically, the Mafia started in Italy, in Sicily, during the mid-1880s. The Sicilians were getting pretty damned tired of every asshole under the sun, from the French to the Spanish to even their own neighbors to the north in mainland Italy invading their bucolic island, stealing their cheese and Chianti, and raping their women. (And who could blame them? How would you feel if some *stronzo* kept stealing your Chianti?) So the Sicilians created a secret society to kick interloper ass and called it *mafiusu*, which translates roughly as "boldness" or "bravado." Of course, if you ask any true-blue wiseguy what the real name of the Mafia is called, he'll tell you it's la Cosa Nostra: meaning "our thing" or sometimes "this thing of ours."

The American Mafia came to power back in the 1920s, when a group of Jewish and Italian immigrants found a golden opportunity to make money: Prohibition. The Volstead Act became law when a bunch of well-meaning fatheads down in Washington decided to make booze illegal for the good of mankind. But they forgot one small item: when a man wants a drink, he'll do anything to get it, even if it's illegal. Seeing this, some smart, tough, and resourceful guys found a way to meet the demands of a thirsty America. It was called bootlegging—and these guys blasted their way to a king's ransom.

Irish mobsters controlled most of the rackets at first, until ambitious and enterprising Italians such as Lucky Luciano and Frank Costello and Jews such as Meyer Lansky and Bugsy Siegel came up out of the slums of New York's Lower East Side. They bumped off the competition and built a criminal empire off the profits of illegal booze. With this bankroll, they moved into the other rackets—loan-sharking, gambling, prostitution, protection, and more—exploiting every vice known to mankind. It's all about teamwork.

Now, if you're too lazy to do any further reading on how the Mafia was born in America, watch both *The Godfather* and *The Godfather Part II.* (Skip the third one—it sucks.) Brando and company pretty much nailed it.

Murder, Inc.

If you were thinking of calling your organization this, fuggedabouddit. The name's been taken, and by stone-cold killers with names like Kid Twist Reles, Tic Toc Tannenbaum, Blue Jaw Magoon, Pugsy Feinstein, Charlie the Bug, and Pittsburgh Phil Strauss, who dispatched his victims with an icepick and once opined, "It's okay to do murder as long as I don't get caught."

Murder, Inc. consisted of a group of the aforementioned Brooklyn thugs and was headed by kill-crazy mob boss Albert Anastasia, who was also known as "the Lord High Executioner" for his readiness to kill anyone, anytime, for any major or minor infraction. Murder, Inc. served as the enforcement arm of the Syndicate—on call 24/7, the boys of Murder, Inc. were responsible for all the killings, dismemberments, and forced vacations, usually permanent, of rivals.

Murder, Inc. fizzled in the early 1940s when Abe "Kid Twist" Reles sang like a canary after he got busted, so he could avoid the electric chair. He exposed more than seventy murders and alluded to hundreds more. It's likely he would have implicated a lot of the higher-ups, such as Bugsy Siegel and Frank Costello and Albert Anastasia, had he not mysteriously fallen to his death from a sixth-floor window at the Half Moon Hotel in Coney Island—and while under the "protection" of six armed police officers. The canary could sing, the mob boys said after hearing the news, but he couldn't fly.

The lesson you can take away from his, well, "fall from grace?" Keep your trap shut. Omertà (see page 51) is sacred; if you become a rat, know that you will be exterminated.

The Top Bananas (and Bonannos)

Organized crime was built by the cunning, resourcefulness, greed, and evil deeds of some very bad boys. (Or some very ambitious and enterprising businessmen, depending on your point of view.) You won't find every mobster that ever lived here—just the big boys, the architects of organized crime in America.

Take It from Me . . .

A mobster can only be killed by those who are close to him. This means they have to be betrayed almost all the time. Therefore, you would be wise not to trust your wife, your children, or even your own mother. Remember the words of Don Corleone: "Keep your friends close, but your enemies closer." Though he should've added, "Unless they don't use deodorant."

First, the Jewish Mobsters

Like I said, Jewish mobsters came first. They did some bad things, they made a shitload of cash, but then they disappeared from the mob scene altogether, because they didn't want their children "in the life."

Meyer Lansky
(born 1902, as Majer Suchowlinski; died 1983)
a.k.a. "the Little Man"

One of Meyer Lansky's biggest claims to fame was that he started the National Crime Syndicate with his old friend from the Lower East Side, Charles "Lucky" Luciano, and later helped consolidate all the mobs both Italian and Jewish across the United States. Lansky's favorite racket was gambling, and he had the market cornered in New York, Florida, and Cuba by the mid 1930s. He was also a big investor in Bugsy Siegel's Flamingo (see page 7), the first of the big Las Vegas hotel-casinos. Together, Siegel and Lansky helped Luciano rise to the pinnacle of Mafia power, dispatching old-time mob bosses, or "moustache Petes" as they were derisively called, such as Salvatore Maranzano and Joe "the Boss" Masseria (see page 12). Luciano's advice to his underworld assoiates was, "Always listen to Meyer." One FBI official grudgingly said of Lansky, "He could have been the head of General Motors if he'd gone into legitimate business."

Of course, he did also have a hand in Siegel's undoing, but we'll get into that a little later.

There's a rumor that Lansky was in possession of photos of J. Edgar Hoover in drag, and this could be the reason Hoover didn't put much effort into hunting down Lansky in particular or organized crime in general. On the other hand, Lansky was an expert at flying below the radar. He never officially owned any property and, after his death, there wasn't a dollar listed anywhere in his name.

For these reasons, Lansky makes a great career criminal to model your own career after—just about the best. He was one of the "lucky ones" after all: when he died in Miami Beach, he wasn't in jail (in fact, he had only served one short sentence in his life); it was natural causes that did him in (lung cancer—at eighty-one!), and he was still reportedly worth $300 million. (To which his widow scoffed, "I'd like to know where all that money is!") The character of Hyman Roth in *The Godfather, Part II*—chillingly portrayed by the late Lee Strasberg—was based on Mr. Lansky.

Benjamin Siegel
(born 1906, as Benjamin Siegelbaum; died 1947)
a.k.a. "Bugsy"

During his fairly short-lived career, Siegel made a name for himself as the world's most famous Jewish hitman. His idea of breakfast was lead and bagels. And when you got a schmear from him, it was your last. The erratic and violent Siegel actually hated being called Bugsy, which essentially means "crazy." Those foolish enough to address Benny as "Bugsy" to his face rarely lived to do it a second time.

He was a childhood friend of Meyer Lansky, and later he, Lansky, and Charles Luciano became bootlegging kings during Prohibition. Lansky was the brains, Siegel was the muscle. In the late 1930s, Siegel was sent to Los Angeles by the Syndicate to keep an eye on its interests out there, specifically to infiltrate the unions that worked for the major movie studios. It was on a trip to Nevada that Siegel discovered a sleepy little town called Las Vegas—you know the rest.

Vegas may have been his claim to fame, but it also became his undoing. When Lansky and Frank Costello and the rest of the Outfit suspected Siegel was skimming mob money from the building of the first big casino, the Flamingo (so named for Siegel's girlfriend, mob moll Virginia Hill, whose nickname was Flamingo), Siegel shot to the top spot on the Syndicate hit list. Most people believe that Bugsy was killed by a bullet shot clean through the eye, but it was actually a bullet through the cheek and nose that did him in.

Is he a good guy to model your career after? That all depends on what you consider important. True, he pretty much invented Las Vegas, and his zeal for partying earned him the title "King of the Sunset Strip." And we can pretty much thank him for "Whatever happens in Vegas, stays in Vegas" (and there are probably hundreds of his own "secrets" buried in shallow graves all over the desert over there). And he did have lots of hot chicks swarming around him all the time. But he made that one mistake that inevitably proves fatal for budding mobsters: he got greedy. And he got caught. I rest my case.

If you take any lesson away from the life and death of Bugsy Siegel, it should be this: stealing from your buddies is a great way to terminate a friendship—with extreme prejudice.

Dutch Schultz
(born 1902, as Arthur Flegenheimer; died 1935)
a.k.a. "the Dutchman"

Revered and feared for his brutal displays of violence, Schultz was one of the meanest, most vicious gangsters of all time.

Born of German Jewish descent in the Bronx, he was arrested early on, and became the bane of the staff at the prison where he was detained, by torturing them mercilessly. He also aggravated them by escaping once or twice.

Schultz reigned as a top bootlegger and alcohol infiltrator of unions, and ran a hugely profitable numbers racket in Harlem, all of which made him a very wealthy man. But in 1935, things started to turn sour. The law was cracking down on the rackets. Schultz found himself in the crosshairs of ambitious Manhattan DA Thomas Dewey. Schultz's solution was simple: kill Dewey. His mob pals, who included Luciano, Lansky, Frank Costello, et al., opposed the move—killing Dewey, they argued, would bring down too much heat on all of them. Schultz defied their hands-off-Dewey edict and thereby sealed his own doom. (Not to mention, mob greed being what it was, Luciano and Co. eyed Schultz's rackets with envy.) Plus, Schultz was a little too fond of inflicting bodily harm at a time when the mob was trying to chill out on the whole violence thing. Dutch had to go.

He was ambushed in the Palace Chophouse in Newark, New Jersey, by a team of Murder, Inc.'s finest (who included Charles "the Bug" Workman and Emanuel "Mendy" Weiss), who opened fire on him and his boys. As legend has it, Dutch was gunned down in the men's crapper. He preferred, however, not to die in a toilet. He managed to drag his bullet-riddled near-corpse out of the bathroom and had someone call an ambulance. He made it to the hospital, where he endured hours of massive surgery; but hours later, he developed peritonitis and died.

Despite his wealth and fearsome reputation, however, the mortally wounded Schultz would become famous for the insane gibberish he muttered to police from his deathbed, while he was delirious from a high fever and hopped up on morphine. Savor these nuggets:

- "A boy has never wept . . . nor dashed a thousand kim"
- "You can play jacks, and girls do that with a soft ball and do tricks with it"
- "Oh, oh, dog biscuit, and when he is happy he doesn't get snappy"

And . . .

- "French Canadian bean soup"

What can you take away from all this? If you're doped up on morphine, don't talk to anyone—especially the heat. You can undo a lifetime of terror and power and respect with French-Canadian bean soup. On the plus side, however, Schultz is credited with the invention of cement shoes—filling a vat with wet cement, plopping his enemies down into it until the stuff dried. The poor schmuck would then be put on a motorboat and unceremoniously dumped overboard. So we all owe the Dutchman for a very effective method of making our enemies disappear permanently.

Arnold Rothstein
(born 1882; died 1928)
a.k.a. "Mr. Big," "the Fixer," "the Man Uptown," "the Big Bankroll," "the Brain"

This famed New York "businessman" was a top bootlegger (he allegedly coined the phrase "Why buy retail, bootlicker, when you can buy it from me wholesale?") during Prohibition, but his main claim to fame is that he was alleged to be the man responsible for fixing the 1919 World Series. He paid off players on the Chicago White Sox to throw the game, and made a ton of cash on the result. F. Scott Fitzgerald based the character Meyer Wolfsheim, Jay Gatsby's shady pal, in *The Great Gatsby*, on Arnold Rothstein.

Widely invested in illicit gambling, narcotics distribution, and virtually every other racket, Rothstein had become a millionaire by age thirty. He was also a popular mediator between rival gangs, for a hefty sum, of course, and is credited by mob historians as the man who invented bootlegging.

Rothstein's career came to an abrupt halt in 1927 over a dispute during a poker game. He refused to pay some $320,000 he had lost because, ironically, he claimed the game had been fixed. A more popular belief, however, was that Dutch Schultz had put a hit on him because Rothstein's protégé, Jack Diamond, had whacked Schultz's friend, Joey Noe. Whatever—nobody in mobdom was too sorry to see Rothstein go. They wanted his rackets. And as usual, they got their way.

What can you learn from him? Well, you don't have to come from a crime family to make it big in the crime biz. Rothstein's father was actually a successful legitimate businessman. Also, though, what comes around goes around. When karma bites back in gangland, it bites hard. Lesson: When you're the king, some asshole will always try to knock you off the throne.

Famous Hits—at a Glance

Name	How?
Bugsy Siegel	Shot through the cheek and nose in the Beverly Hills home he shared with Virginia Hill.
Dutch Schultz	Blasted while taking a whiz in a Newark, New Jersey, restaurant.
Arnold Rothstein	Shot by parties unknown in 1927 at the Park-Central Hotel in midtown Manhattan; died the following day.
Albert Anastasia	Clipped by the kill-crazy Gallo brothers while he enjoyed a shave in a barber chair, almost thirty years to the day after Arnold Rothstein's execution—and in the same location, the Park Central Hotel.
Salvatore Maranzano	Clipped in his Park Avenue office by two wiseguys posing as policemen, in 1931. Lucky Luciano, Meyer Lansky, Frank Costello, Bugsy Siegel, and Tommy "Three Fingers" Lucchese were the men who masterminded the hit, because Maranzano wanted all the "young turks" out of the way. He also disapproved of Luciano and Costello doing business with "those Jews." *(continued on next page)*

Name	How?
Joe Masseria	Assassinated in 1931 at the Nuova Villa Tammaro restaurant in Coney Island while dining with Lucky Luciano. When asked by the cops where he was at the time of the murder, Luciano said, "I was in the bathroom taking a leak. I take a long leak."
Joseph "Crazy Joe" Gallo	Whacked at his own birthday party at Umberto's Clam House in New York City's Little Italy.
Sam Giancana	Murdered while frying up sausage and peppers in the basement of his Oak Park, Illinois, home.

The Italian Invasion

It's not one hundred percent accurate to say that the Italians "took over" organized crime from the Jews; it's more like they swooped in and had more staying power. Initially, both groups worked in tandem. But, unlike how it was with the Italians, as Jewish wiseguys began dropping off, no one else wanted to take their places.

"I was in the bathroom taking a leak. I take a long leak."

—Lucky Luciano, when asked by cops where he was at the time of Joe Masseria's death

Al Capone

(born 1899, as Alphonse Gabriel Capone; died 1947)
a.k.a. "Scarface"

Al Capone, probably the most infamous gangster in American history, is usually portrayed as a homicidal, cigar-chomping monster. The sinister-looking slash across his cheek (compliments of brute Frank Gallucio, whom he later hired as a bodyguard) didn't help. Capone brought a bloodthirsty savagery to the Mafia that even shocked his old friends back east.

Brooklyn-born to immigrants, Capone began his life of crime in New York before relocating to Chicago in 1919 at the request of another Brooklyn-born mobster, Johnny Torrio, who needed a man of Al's talents. There, he became a capo in charge of many of the booze and prostitution rackets in the city. Chicago was "his kind of town." Also, he was wanted back in New York for questioning in a couple of murders. Al decided to stick around the Windy City.

If you're looking to follow in his footsteps, study the details of his biggest success: the 1929 Saint Valentine's Day Massacre on Chicago's North Side. It's still the biggest bloodbath in gangland history—seven members of rival bootlegger Bugs Moran's gang were lined up against a garage wall and machine-gunned by Capone hitters dressed as cops. Fed up with their city being turned into a war zone, the good people of Chicago demanded Capone's head on a platter.

But it wasn't rival gangsters or even the cops that brought Scarface down. It was the bean counters at the IRS.

Now as role models go, you could do a lot worse than Capone. He ruled his criminal empire with an iron fist and whacked anyone who dared challenge him. However, you need to avoid repeating his biggest fuck-up. Although Capone survived many assassination attempts, he ultimately got pinched for tax evasion and was handed a sentence of eleven-plus years.

In his later years, Capone's mental capacity started to seriously deteriorate due to the syphilis he contracted when he was young, which for some reason was never treated. In 1947, Capone had a stroke, which he survived. But then a few days later, he contracted pneumonia and died. Capone Lesson #1: If you like to bang the bimbos—and who doesn't?—just be careful where you stick your *sausage*. Catching a STD these days is as easy as ordering a pizza.

Perhaps the biggest lesson you can learn from Capone's life and career is to make sure you hire a damned good accountant to look after your finances. That, and the fact that a little antibiotics will go a long way.

"Only Capone kills like that!"

—Bugs Moran, after hearing seven of his boys
were cut down

Albert Anastasia
(born 1902, as Umberto Anastasio; died 1957)
a.k.a. "the Mad Hatter," "Lord High Executioner"

Albert Anastasia represented himself as a legitimate businessman, giving himself the title of "sales representative" for the Convertible Mattress Corporation in Brooklyn, New York. Of course, even in a time of a mob war, when every wiseguy in town is "going to the mattresses," there was no way an everyday salesman could amass the fortune Anastasia did.

Anastasia loved to kill and would do so at the slightest provocation. Which is why being one of the founding members of Murder, Inc. was such a natural fit for him. And thanks to Albert and his passion for bloodshed, his buddy, Charles "Lucky" Luciano, was able to become the boss of bosses. Still,

Anastasia was a loose cannon and required a lot of supervision.

With a little help from his friends (who had their own interests to consider), Anastasia eventually became boss of his own family. And that's when his bloodlust went off the charts.

When Anastasia started behaving erratically, ordering hits on anyone for slights real and imagined, his days became numbered. Ruthless mobster Vito Genovese began using Anastasia's antics to turn his supporters against him. Don Vito, sensing weakness at the top ranks of the Mafia leadership (Luciano was deported back to his native Sicily in 1948 and Frank Costello was trying to distance himself from la Cosa Nostra) knew that only Albert Anastasia stood between him and his long-standing desire to become *capodi tutti de capi*, the boss of bosses.

In 1957, as Anastasia sat in a barber chair at the Park Sheraton Hotel, two men wearing scarves on their faces rushed in and ambushed him. In his confusion, Anastasia started firing at the mirror, unaware he was shooting at his killers' reflections.

What you can learn from this: Anastasia was losing his grip. A staunch Luciano/Costello loyalist, Albert A. ignored the warning signs that Genovese was moving against him. The troublemaking but shrewd Genovese (a huge fan of Machiavelli) started by turning Anastasia's allies against him, convincing them that Albert A. was bad for business. The Mad Hatter never saw it coming. The moral is, never stop looking over your shoulder and always keep a wet finger on the winds of change. Your life depends on it.

John Gotti
(born 1940; died 2002)
a.k.a. "Dapper Don," "the Teflon Don"

Although many who came before him inspired Hollywood films and wiseguy characters, it was John Gotti who really turned

Mafia bosses into movie stars. He became a celebrity. His notoriety made the "Gotti" name a brand name in organized crime, and his fame—it was world wide. Even six years after his death, more people know his name than those of their own senators.

Gotti started out as a regular guy, working as a coat factory presser and a truck driver's assistant, but got fed up being a working stiff who lived paycheck to paycheck. In 1966, he became an associate of New York's Gambino crime family, under the tutelage of old-time mobster Aniello "Mr. Neil" Dellacroce, who had an eye for young talent. Gotti made his bones in the Gambino family by rubbing out—in front of a dozen witnesses in a Staten Island bar—an Irish hoodlum named James McBratney, who had allegedly kidnapped Carlo Gambino's nephew and killed him, even though the ransom had been paid. Gotti went to prison and did his stretch without complaint. When he was released, it was merely a matter of time (and one very well-planned assassination) before he hit the big time.

His big break came when the family boss, Paul Castellano, wanted Gotti's crew disbanded because they were allegedly running drugs and the big boss didn't approve. They got even. In December 1985, Castellano and his bodyguard were shot down in front of New York City's Sparks Steak House, in a double hit that has become the stuff of Mafia legend for its planning and—you'll pardon the expression—its execution. Gotti was now the head of the Gambino family.

The city of New York and the feds in DC tried three times to bring him down, and failed. He got the nickname "the Teflon Don" because no charges would stick.

Ultimately, though, Gotti was knocked off his perch. He was picked up on a bunch of FBI wiretaps, discussing family business at his social club in Little Italy. Also, Gotti began enjoying his newfound celebrity a little too much—keeping a low profile is essential in the mob—and began flaunting his fame and power and reveling in his celebrity status. It was pretty much the same scenario that brought down Lucky Luciano half a century earlier.

So, what we can learn from John Gotti? Simple: To make it to the top of the mob heap, you need (1) balls like coconuts, (2) eyes like a hawk, and (3) nerves of steel.

What you can learn from his failures? Beware of FBI wiretaps. Even if you've swept your hangout a dozen times for bugs, make it a habit to check two or three times a day. Also, don't get too cocky, at least in the media. When you make *Time* magazine's Man of the Year, you're probably getting way too much publicity.

Salvatore Maranzano
(born 1868; died 1931)
a.k.a. "the Boss of Bosses"

No one would ever have dreamed of calling this guy "Father Sal," although there was a time in his life, while still in Italy, that he actually played with the idea of becoming a priest. Instead, he moved to the United States, set up and grew a bootleg liquor business, and then started to invade the interests of other career criminals . . .

Throughout his career, Maranzano embodied opulence, formality, and being civilized. He had a hand in the murder of Joe Masseria (see page 18) and eventually became boss. His days were numbered, however; his reign lasted only five months.

It's one thing to be arrogant when you're boss, but you want to have some tact, especially with people you deem as your underlings. Not everyone you see as an underling will necessarily think of themselves this way.

When Maranzano got it into his head that he should become the supreme leader, he made a lot of enemies, Charles Luciano and Joe Bonanno among them. He sanctioned hits on them and on others he perceived as threats, but Lucky and his boys beat him to the draw.

You know the phrase that the only things certain in life are death and taxes? No one knew that better than Sal Maranzano, who was whacked by Jewish mobsters (so Maranzano wouldn't recognize them) disguised as New York's Finest and specially trained for the murder detail by Meyer Lansky and Bugsy Siegel.

What can you take away from this? Ambition, if not properly managed, can get you dead.

Joe Masseria
(born c. 1869, as Giuseppe Masseria; died 1931)
a.k.a. "Joe the Boss," "Joe the Pig," "Big Guy"

Masseria may have been in charge of all organized crime from 1920 to his death in 1931, but his biggest claim to fame was his gluttony. "The guy ate like he had two assholes," one old wiseguy remembered. So when he was lured out for a lavish ten-course lunch and to play cards with Charles "Lucky" Luciano at Nuova Villa Tammaro restaurant in Coney Island, it was an offer he couldn't refuse.

Lucky stuffed Joe the Boss with pasta, veal, chicken, and sausage, all washed down with a gallon of Chianti. "He was such a pig," Luciano wrote in his autobiography, "he ate with his hands." Lucky suggested a game of pinnocle, all the while plying Fat Joe with more wine. At some point during the game, Luciano excused himself to go to the men's room, and the hit team arrived, among them Vito Genovese and Bugsy Siegel. They put the big blast on Joe the Boss.

What can be said about Joe Masseria? Pigs get fat and hogs get slaughtered. Or maybe the main lesson here is that you should never play cards with a guy named Lucky.

Charles Luciano
(born 1897; died 1962)
a.k.a. "Lucky"

Born in Sicily, "Lucky" Luciano immigrated with his family to the United States in 1907; that same year, at the ripe old age of ten, he took his first pinch for shoplifting.

By 1930, Luciano had established himself as a respected player in the national crime syndicate he and Meyer Lansky had created. Old "Moustache Petes" like Salvatore Maranzano (who considered himself the "boss of bosses" after Masseria's death) had to go. Why did Lucky turn against his onetime business associate? Maranzano ordered a hit on Luciano, who was then abducted and taken to a remote spot on Staten Island where he was beaten, slashed, and left for dead. Lucky lived, however, and was a whole lot wiser as a result.

That Luciano survived being "taken for a ride," he became something of a legend, the man they couldn't kill. Backed by Lansky, Costello, and most of the Italian Mafia membership, Luciano knocked off both Masseria and Maranzano and became the head of a nationwide crime syndicate whose remnants are still in place today.

In 1936, however, Luciano was tried and convicted and sentenced to fifty years in the slammer for being the mastermind behind a citywide prostitution ring. Many mob historians claim it was a bum rap—Manhattan district attorney Thomas Dewey, eager to get Lucky for anything and politically ambitious, trumped up the charges and paraded out a bunch of old whores (with names like Cokey Flo) who claimed Lucky beat them and forced them into becoming two-dollar-a-trick hookers. The jury believed them.

During World War II, the army allegedly enlisted Lucky's help to use the Mafia to protect the New York City waterfront from German saboteurs. Using his Mafia connections, Lucky is also credited with aiding the American invasion of Sicily during the war, providing intelligence. In exchange, Luciano was eventually paroled in 1946, under the condition that he be deported to Sicily and never return to the United States. But return he did in 1964, after his death, to be buried in Queens. Lucky always got the last laugh.

The biggest lesson to be learned here is that you have to create your own luck. Because, despite his nickname, Charlie Lucky Luciano made it to the top of the Mafia the old-fashioned way—hard work, determination, guts, and the ability to step over a lot of dead bodies. In short, all the skills you need to start your own Mafia family. However . . .

Lucky had one weakness: he loved seeing his name in the newspapers. He reveled in his reputation of being the biggest gangster (after Capone's downfall) in the world. Being in the spotlight is great if you're a movie star or a sports hero. If you're a gangster, though, flaunting your fame as Luciano did only attracts the unwanted attention of the government watchdogs and district attorneys. Being Public Enemy #1 is great for the ego but it ultimately led to Lucky's downfall in 1936. And in mobdom, history does repeat itself—the lust for fame is also what would bring John Gotti down half a century later. The lesson to be learned here is: Pride goeth before a fall. If you're gonna be a mob boss, keep your mug out of the newspapers and off the TV.

Frank Costello
(born 1891, as Francesco Castiglia; died 1973)

Can you fuck up big time and still rise to the top in the Mafia? Mistakes in the mob usually lead to erasure but, every now and then, the mob gods shine down on you, which is what happened when Vito Genovese ordered a hit on beloved crime boss, Frank Costello.

With Lucky Luciano deported to Italy and Albert Anastasia dead, Frank Costello found himself alone and in the crosshairs of Vito Genovese's gunsights. Genovese was angling for the boss of bosses gig and Frank Costello was the only one standing in his way. He dispatched a hitman, Vinnie "the Chin" Gigante to do the job. Fortunately for Costello, Gigante botched the job, only creasing Costello's scalp with the bullet. Some mob experts believe Gigante meant to miss, to serve as a warning to Costello that it was time to retire. Costello took the hint and turned over most of his rackets to Genovese. And bided his time. A few years later, Costello, Meyer Lansky, and Lucky Luciano, in a maneuver Machiavelli would have been proud of, set up Genovese to get popped in a major drug bust. Genovese spent the rest of his life behind bars.

Joseph Gallo
(born 1929; died 1972)
a.k.a. "Joey," "Crazy Joe"

How bad of a criminal are you when other criminals see you as dangerous? If you're the kind of guy who's so crazy, even your friends and family dread you, then you may consider "Crazy" Joe Gallo as the perfect role model.

Uncontrollable by his own Red Hook, Brooklyn, gang (which included his brother Larry), Gallo answered to no one and feared no man. He was a stone-cold killer and, many mob scholars say, a total fucking psychotic (solid attributes for leading your own crime family)—he thought nothing of taking on the very family he worked for, the Profacis (later the Colombos), in a mob war that littered the streets of Brooklyn with dead wiseguys on both sides. What Crazy Joe wanted was a bigger piece of the pie. Problem was, Don Joe Profaci didn't want to share with *stronzos* like Joey Gallo and his band of Red Hook Robin Hoods.

Crazy Joe survived a number of assassination attempts but, before the Profaci hitters could take him out, the law saved them the trouble, sentencing him to ten years in the slammer for extortion. When he came out, Crazy Joe was—on the surface, anyway—a changed man. He became the darling of the New York literary set and wrote poetry, in an effort to appear legit. At heart, though, he was still a wiseguy.

The "problem child" of the Profaci family finally got his due. Crazy Joe didn't give a shit that he was the subject of a mob manhunt with orders to shoot to kill. On April 7, 1972, his forty-third birthday, he was celebrating at a party thrown in his honor at Umberto's Clam House in Little Italy, when three uninvited guests stormed in and filled him full of lead. Crazy Joe went face down into his fried calamari but summoned the strength to stumble out onto Mulberry Street in pursuit of the shooters. He died minutes later.

The lesson here is simple: If you're gonna be crazy in the mob, at least be smart about it. Joey Gallo pissed off a lot of very dangerous mafiosi. There was a $50,000 contract out on his ass, yet he shrugged off the threat and went to dinner in Little Italy, which was crawling with wiseguys eager to bag Crazy Joe and claim that $50 large. Which is ultimately what happened.

The bottom line here is, don't make yourself a target like Crazy Joe did.

Zaza!

The character of Joey Zaza in *The Godfather Part III* (played to perfection by Joe Mantegna) was based in large part on Joey Gallo, with a little John Gotti tossed in for good measure.

Carlo Gambino
(born 1902; died 1976)

If you're not looking for a lot of drama, don't mind other wise-guys grabbing all the headlines, want to make untold millions, and find the idea of dying peacefully of old age in your own bed appealing, then Carlo Gambino is the man to copy. He ruled during the golden era of the Mafia—the time in which the mob was the most powerful (the 1960s to 1970s)—yet the public at large barely knew of him, even though he ran the most powerful and feared Mafia family in America—a family that to this day proudly carries the name of Gambino.

Just because the meek-looking and introspective Gambino kept a low profile, though, don't think he was a pushover. Far from it—he was shrewd, cunning, and didn't hesitate to order killings whenever necessary. (Gambino and Vito Genovese masterminded the barbershop hit on Albert Anastasia, which cleared the way for Carlo to take over *la famiglia*.)

The lesson to be learned from Carlo Gambino—and it's a damn good one—is, don't be in such a frigging rush. Takes time to make it to the top, especially when your competition is a lot bigger and tougher than you are. Carlo was content (or pretended to be content) being number two to Anastasia, who was known to slap little Carlo around on occasion to get his jollies. Gambino didn't complain. When the time was right—in 1957—he slapped back, and Albert Anastasia became just another one of the honored dead in the annals of the Mafia.

Joseph Bonanno
(born 1905 as Giuseppe Bonanno; died 2002)
a.k.a. "Joe the Boss," "Joe Bananas"

Unlike many other wiseguys, Bonanno was a multimillionaire who actually made some of his fortune legitimately in real estate, funeral homes, the garment industry, and cheese factories. But just some . . . He also helped his family prosper in less-legit pursuits, such as loan-sharking, bookmaking, numbers running, and prostitution.

By the 1950s and 1960s, most of his good friends and allies had either been whacked or arrested, which left the door wide open for foul play. Bonanno was kidnapped by a Buffalo crime family and held captive for a while until his son, Salvatore, started a war to get him back, which is commonly referred to as "the Banana War."

He died of natural causes at ninety-seven. What can we learn from Joe Bonanno? When the other mobs are lined up against you and tell you it's time to retire—then retire. *Capisce?*

Sam Giancana
(born Momo Salvatore Guingano in 1908; died 1975)
a.k.a. "Momo," "Mo," "Mooney," "Sam the Cigar"

Sam Giancana was as in-your-face as they come in the wiseguy world, and his excessive, high-profile antics eventually led to him having to step down from the post of boss in 1966.

Giancana was a Chicago crime boss who had pull throughout the country, including ties with JFK and other powerful folks. He wore dark sunglasses all the time, and allegedly also bedded Marilyn Monroe and got Sinatra his part in *From Here to Eternity*. But rubbing elbows and other body parts with the rich and famous and powerful and connected doesn't mean you're going to be home free.

He also had serious legal problems, which caused him to live in exile in Mexico after stepping down. For seven years, the Mexican government tried to get rid of him and, once they were successful, he returned to the United States and was promptly shot to death. Somehow, the gunmen managed to get by the FBI surveillance team and Chicago police guarding Giancana at the time.

What you can learn from this is simple: If your enemies want you dead, they'll find a way. It doesn't matter who you are or who you know. When your number's up, they're going to get you.

Film and TV Mobsters, Part 1

As you start seriously thinking about putting your plan into action and assembling your own crime family, here are some of the flicks that are essential to your success. The lessons you'll learn can be invaluable, and might even prolong your life.

Scarface

Scarface can be the bible for you if want to adopt a "take it, it's yours" cowboy mentality. Yes, Tony Montana is fearless, but he's also insane, snorts too much coke, and has a very unhealthy attachment to his own sister. It ably demonstrates how craziness is tolerated—up to a point—in organized crime. So fine, follow some of Tony's antics if you must, but for your own health and well-being, take it down a notch.

GoodFellas

Tommy DeSimone (played by Joe Pesci) is a great example of how you can start at the bottom, kill your way up the ladder of mob success, and then end up in some wiseguy's rec room with a bullet in your head. Martin Scorsese's *GoodFellas* is the ultimate mob flick, showing the everyday workings of a real crime family, the deceits and double-crosses, and how wiseguys become stool pigeons. It's also a primer on how to avoid ending up in the back of a garbage truck, on a meathook, or head first into a pizza oven.

(continued on next page)

Bugsy

Warren Beatty was way too old to play Bugsy Siegel, who was only forty-one when he was whacked, but Bugsy's message is crystal clear: No man is bigger than the crime syndicate that spawned him. Fuck up enough times and your best friend will put a contract out on you.

Closing Thoughts

Whether you base your mobster persona on a real-life wiseguy or a screen thug, you have to study the guts as well as the glory. If you decide to ignore the hard lessons of those gangsters who went prematurely to their graves—some in twenty or more different pieces—then you have no one but yourself to blame when you're dumped into a lake or an ocean with a jukebox tied around your neck.

CHAPTER 2

Living the Mobster Life

or,

Take the Gun, Leave the Cannoli

To me, being a wiseguy was better than being president of the United States.
—Henry Hill, in *Wiseguy* by Nick Pileggi

SURE, I KNOW YOU WANNA BE A WISEGUY—WHY THE HELL ELSE WOULD you be reading this now if you didn't? But there are a couple of things you need to know before we begin. For starters, being a wiseguy isn't a job, it's not even a career—it's 100 percent commitment, which is why being in the mob is often referred to as being "in the life."

Being a successful mobster means putting "the life" before everything—before your wife, your kids, your mistress (or mistresses).

So decide here and now before proceeding with this book. If you can't dedicate yourself to a life of stealing, killing, maiming, and dismembering your enemies or exploiting those weaker than you are, and honest civilians alike, close this book now. If you're not willing to be feared instead of loved and don't have the stomach for violence—walk away before it's too late. No hard feelings and nothing to be ashamed of. Not everyone is able to work over a rival wiseguy with a cattle prod to his balls or dismember a dead person with a chainsaw or give some unsuspecting slob a 9 mm headache . . .

In this chapter, I'll show you what it means to be a gentleman—and a savage—as we walk through a mobster's typical day. You'll get tips on how to dress, what to eat, what to drive, and more.

Take It from Me . . .

It's essential to have a vice, one that you wrestle with on a daily basis. Whether it's drinking or gambling or excessive womanizing—even cigars or suicidal amounts of fettuccine alla Bolognese and sausage with peppers—the struggle to control your vices will keep you from getting soft, both mentally and physically.

In this chapter, you will:

- Nail down a wiseguy alias for yourself and also learn how to create nicknames for your crew
- Learn the essential elements of a mobster's wardrobe
- Witness a day in the life of a real wiseguy

"Are youse alone, or are youse by yourself?"

—Benny "the Omelet" Manganari to
Albert "Little Chinky" Vitali, FBI wiretap,
Brooklyn, New York, 1987

The Mobster Mystique

It's no wonder so many people set out to become mobsters every year. The perks are incredible. Your new BMW just ran out of gas? No problem. Buy another one with a full tank—in cash. You get to have every judge, politician, and police chief in your pocket whenever those pain-in-the-ass good-government groups start sniffing around. And let's not forget having an extremely obedient and, uh, "flexible" lawyer at your disposal. On top of all that, you get to have a really cool nickname. And what's more fun than that? (See below.)

On the downside, being a Mafia don involves a lot of stress. On top of being CEO of a major operation, you're always in the position of having to watch your back. You have to stay on top of the latest trends. You have to juggle all those women. Seriously. Poor guy.

What's in a Nickname?

Nicknames are essential in Mafia society. Everyone should have one, and that alias should inspire fear, dread, alarm, respect—all at once.

Typically, you don't get to choose your own nickname. In a traditional Mafia family, it gets chosen for you. Lucky for you, however, you're not part of a traditional Italian Mafia family. You're starting the thing, so choose the alias you want to go by. Your alias is part of the legend you are in the process of creating, so go hog wild.

Your underlings are also yours for the naming. You have the power to call those who report to you whatever you choose. Italian-American comic Rich Franchese does a great bit on how Italians get their nicknames. He says that, unlike other people who might get their nicknames for something they might be extremely proud of or in a

(continued on next page)

positive way, Italians give nicknames to other Italians because of handicaps and other attributes. For example:

- Anthony is 400 pounds, so he's called "Fat Tony."
- Ralph got his ear sliced off in a fight—he becomes "Ralphie One-Ear."
- One of Mike's legs is shorter than the other—meet "Mikey the Cripple."
- Joey had to be rushed to the hospital after swallowing too many meatballs—introducing "Joey Meatballs."

However, a Mafia nickname can also be given for positive attributes, or at least for non-negative ones. A good example is the character of Salvatore "Big Pussy'" Bonpensiero on *The Sopranos*. One might think this nickname came about because Bomp was a fat coward, but this is wrong. Vincent Pastore's character is based on a real New Jersey mobster who got the nickname because (1) he was overweight, and (2) he was a first-rate cat burglar. He also had a baby brother who aided and abetted the burglaries, so they became, respectively, Big Pussy and Little Pussy.

Keep in mind that although it can be a lot of fun to shoulder your subordinates with ridiculous monikers, you do have an image to present to the outside world, and you need to take that into account. You probably wouldn't tremble with terror if Angelo the Tree Toad had a beef with you. But a name like Vinny the Executioner just begs respect.

Nicknames are especially handy during phone conversations when you have to communicate vital, confidential information to your underlings and confuse the law who are likely wiretapping your phone. You say: "Meet me at the joint downtown and bring the Nose and the Meatball." To even the most seasoned cop or FBI agent, you've just spouted a lot of gibberish, but what you've really done is call a meeting with Angelo, Paulie, and Ralph at some Italian restaurant.

Here are some do's and don'ts:

Correct	Incorrect
Joey Meatballs	Joey English Muffins
Benny the Snake	Benny the Titmouse
Mikey the Undertaker	Mikey the CPA
Fat Tony	Overweight Tony
Little Bobby	Vertically Challenged Bobby
Mickey from Flatbush	Mickey from Dayton, Ohio
Sammy the Shark	Sammy the Chilean Seabass

And please note: Every gang should include at least one member named "Crazy."

Starting the Typical Day

When you're a Mafia don, your day starts whenever you feel the hell like waking up. You're not on the clock, you *are* the clock. Everybody and everything revolves around your schedule. Your crew must be made aware that this means you are entitled to call them on a business matter at any time of the morning—whether that means two A.M., six A.M., or both.

Once you get out of bed, it's time to get dressed (we'll go through what to wear a bit later in this chapter) and then head out to enjoy the most important meal of the day. Before leaving your house, however, don't forget to give your wife the information she needs to plan her day—meaning, plan around yours. "I won't be home tonight for dinner," "I will be home tonight for dinner," "I'll be late," "I won't be coming home at all," and so forth. You have to let her know. After all, the last thing you need is for your wife to file a missing persons report with the cops when you're in bed with your *goomar*.

Now that you've gotten that out of the way, head out to your favorite café, where you have ten percent of the interest, and start your day with a double espresso and a hard cookie (they may call this a *biscotti*).

Breakfast is not a time to sit back and relax, however. You'll be putting all that caffeine and sugar to work while scouting out new business opportunities. Read the papers while you enjoy your hard cookie, and see how the competition is doing—friends and enemies. Who got pinched. Who's in the can. Keeping on top of this kind of information is vital to the success of your operation.

Take It from Me . . .

For the most up-to-date mob gossip, log on to Jerry Capeci's Web site, www.ganglandnews.com. It's an invaluable source of all late-breaking mob news—no wiseguy worth his marinara sauce misses it. It's updated every Thursday by Mr. Capeci himself, who for years covered the crime/Mafia beat for the *New York Daily News* and currently the *New York Sun*. And if you see *your* name on Capeci's Web site, call your lawyer ASAP.

Business as Usual

Once you have all the information you need, it's time to check in on your business interests and concentrate on networking. Keep on top of this stuff. Remember: Businesses, especially the small independent variety, come and go. Sure, you can shake down your local delicatessen or convenience store for a few shitty dollars or you can put the bite on their distributors for every quart of milk or carton of cigarettes they deliver.

You'll also need to make time to meet with various members of your crew for updates on current income sources and potential income. This is your most active time of day, as you'll probably need to make a few stops at different places to give your associates the necessary encouragement or discouragement where needed. Be sure to plan accordingly.

This is Joey Sausage. Try telling him he can't park next to a fire hydrant. Every Mafia crew needs at least one guy who looks like this. (photo courtesy David Garofalo)

Then it's time for lunch.

For the most part, lunchtime is spent at your favorite Italian restaurant, where you dine on semolina bread dipped in olive oil, fresh mozzarella, veal scalloppine, chicken Marsala, and spaghetti carbonara.

In a pinch, or in the event you don't have a neighborhood Italian joint, an Olive Garden will do (but only as a last resort).

Now is your time to relax with other made guys, as you play poker, exchange dumb stories about your kids, and brag about the big scores you've made and the women you've banged or are currently banging, and catch up on who's gotten pinched or paroled or whacked.

Your Social Club

Chances are, there isn't an existing "social club" in your neighborhood, but that's good. It could mean the neighborhood is yours for the taking.

Your first step is to find an empty storefront on your town's busiest street. Then you throw in a couple of folding card tables and a dozen or so wood-backed chairs. (It's important to keep the place fairly uncomfortable, to keep your crew from sitting on their asses all day and playing cards when they should be out doing scores or setting up same.)

What should you be looking for as you choose your spot? For one, it should be in a neighborhood you're familiar with, preferably one where you are the "king." This means the local store owners know and respect you. Not only can you have a monetary interest, then, in what comes in and out of your club, but you'll also have a short commute between work and play.

Take It from Me . . .

You don't want to be too close to the local police precinct, for obvious reasons. Keep the heat out of walking—or running—distance. Of course, it's okay to be by a firehouse, because everyone loves firemen. To my knowledge, firemen haven't infiltrated the Mafia.

Other considerations of where your social club is located are that it's convenient to have your lawyer and your goomar within walking distance—no more than ten minutes to either of these, if you can help it. You should also be able to hit the nearest OTB with a baseball.

Outside the social club, there should be plenty of parking for all your oversized vehicles. Inside, it's mandatory that the location have a back door for quick exits, as well as a basement, which you will use for disciplining underlings, and splitting dividends, or in extreme cases, dismembering a body.

After you've established the "where," it's time to focus on "how." When one enters a social club, one should not be sure whether one has walked into a delicatessen, a Vegas card room, or a hunting lodge. The ambience should embody all three.

The fully equipped kitchen will feature card tables, and somewhere there will be a giant TV with every cable channel imaginable—and featuring a sports package.

Finishing touches to the decor may include pictures of Frank Sinatra and the pope, as well as an assortment of Italian sports heroes, like Joe Dimaggio. There should be a cigar humidor—fully stocked—as well as a bar that contains all the finest Italian liqueurs, including Frangelico, Sambuca, Galliano, and grappa

(Sicilian moonshine). And don't forget the espresso machine, although these can be expensive when you're just starting out. So a Mr. Coffee will do for the time being.

Other important considerations include having plenty of video surveillance for the grounds, for your own protection, as well as an amply stocked gun case. For hunting season, of course.

Naming Your Social Club

As we discussed, you've found a deserted storefront on Main Street. You stocked it with a bunch of cheap Kmart chairs and a crappy card table.

When it comes to picking a name for your social club, choose wisely. You don't want to call it Bobby's Mafia Hangout or something dumb-ass like that. John Gotti had his own little sanctuary in Howard Beach, Queens. He called it the Bergin Hunt and Fish Club.

What's really interesting is, none of Gotti's crew would be caught dead near a fishing rod. We're talking about guys with names like "Tony Roach" Rampino, land-locked guys who hated the beach and any water with salt in it. Hunting is another story—Gotti's boys loved to hunt, but their targets were usually human. But it sounded good—hunt and fish, how much more fucking American can you get?

The point is, pick a name that won't attract the attention of cops or any pain-in-the-ass district attorneys. A name that's patriotic or at least gets with the damned program, like The Main Street Monopoly Club. (Wiseguys love Monopoly. It's fun and no one gets hurt—unless you land on Boardwalk with a hotel on it and ain't got the ready cash to pay off the $2,000. Wiseguys have gotten killed for less.)

Here are some acceptable names for your social club:

- The Friends of Italian Opera
- The [Your Town Here] Athletic League

- The Sons of Corleone Social Club
- The Calamari Trading Company
- The Tony Bennett Appreciation Society

Some bad names for a social club:

- The Stay-the-Fuck-Out Social Club
- We're Mobbed-up. You're Not. Go Away.
- The Maple Street Thieves and Murderers Society
- Central Avenue Shakedown and Extortion, Ltd.
- The He-Man Woman-Haters Club

Afternoon Activities

After lunch, it's time to head to the track, where you can play the ponies. Your stature and influence will help you acquire many good horse tips. Depending on how powerful you are, you may also influence the outcome of a race.

Take It from Me . . .

One day, you may own a horse of your own. This is a good thing to aspire to, as it is a sign of status in a mob community—like an Irish guy owning a bar or a Jewish guy owning a deli. It's a sure sign that you have arrived.

After the track, you'll have some time to kill (or maybe some one to kill), before you head home for dinner with the family.

Whatever the case may be, it's likely that all this hard work has tightened your muscles and put you in serious need of a steam bath and massage. Go crazy. There's nothing girlie about a massage, especially if some hot young broad will be working her hands and fingers all over you. And if you're seeing your goomar tonight, don't forget the manicure.

Family Time

Actually, a massage and steam bath are essential precursors to going home for dinner with the family. This is your opportunity to catch up on family matters, and it's not always a pretty sight.

In a traditional Italian family, it's a long-standing tradition that "dinnertime" is actually "family therapy time." As you feign interest in who's on the honor roll and who's in detention, again, try to keep your cool. It's just not worth undoing all that magic fingerwork—and whatever other bonus you enjoyed from your masseuse—to get too upset about home matters. If you feel like you might be reaching overboil at stupid stories of who's been thrown out of little league or how bad someone's math teacher happens to suck—think of all the money you're saving by never needing any outside counseling.

But forget overboiling: The most important thing to remember is to try not to overeat. Explain to your wife that you're counting calories. She will know better, and likely, so will your kids, but once the smoke has cleared on other inevitable blowouts—like your son's fascination with the FBI or daughter's new boyfriend—do you really need to go stirring up any more fires because you can't save yourself from explaining that you're saving room for your second dinner with your mistress?

> *Take It from Me . . .*
> The easiest way to clinch "your table" is by consistent overtipping, but being a "silent partner" at your favorite restaurant is always the safest bet.

Your Spot

This should go without saying, but in case you're harboring any false hope: your goomar don't cook. The women in your life have their roles, and these will be specifically spelled out for you later on. As a rule, never hint, ask, or otherwise suggest to your goomar that she don an apron for her favorite don and whip up a pasta fazool. This will likely lead to a tantrum on her part, perhaps an airborne frying pan ("Of course I know what this is for, you bastard!"), or even withholding of sexual favors on her part. And then what good will she be?

You take that pretty young thing of yours to your favorite restaurant, where you'll sit at "your table," located in the most secluded spot of the restaurant. Don't let her eat too much pasta, though. Sure, she'll need the carbs for the strenuous workout she'll be enduring under or over you later, but you don't want food to go to her luscious hips—or prevent all the wine from going to her head.

It should go without saying that your favorite restaurant be one that you have some level of business interest in—either you're a partner here, or, at the very least, the establishment uses your restaurant supply racket, your liquor distribution, et cetera. Also, it should be made abundantly clear to the owner that he doesn't want trouble with your or any of his deliveries or pickups. That usually does the trick. If he's still too dense to get it, have one of your capos send a soldier to pay him a visit and deliver the message with a clearer, visual, and downright physical presentation.

And remember: The decision to go home to the wife and kids is optional. You either go home or you don't. What isn't optional, however, is telling the wife before you leave the house for the evening what your plans are.

Wardrobe Essentials

Here's a checklist of the staples of any self-respecting wiseguy's closet:

- ❑ An ample supply of wife-beaters—the sleeveless undershirts made famous by Sonny Corleone in *The Godfather*.
- ❑ At least a dozen tailored suits, from sharkskin to basic gray pinstripes. The rule here? The gaudier, the better. After all, Al Capone's favorite suit was lime green with pinstripes.
- ❑ At least a couple of cashmere sports jackets.
- ❑ An assortment of mock turtlenecks.
- ❑ At least a dozen pairs of Italian-made shoes—lace-ups and loafers.
- ❑ A pair of "workboots" for hole digging, dismembering, or other activities that could ruin your good shoes.
- ❑ Several trenchcoats and overcoats. You need an overcoat that can keep you nice and warm in the winter, but don't overlook how easy it makes concealing a weapon or any "borrowed" goods you may have on you. Hart, Shaffner, and Marx have some nice ones.
- ❑ Boxers or briefs? The choice is yours, as always.

What to Wear

As a mobster, you sometimes have to be loud and you always should try to dress loud.

The mobster uniform can be flexible, but only to a point. There are certain articles of clothing that are mandatory, and others that a mobster should never be caught dead in. But Rule No. 1 is to wear Italian-made clothes whenever possible.

Most important, however, is that your free or extremely discounted clothes will reflect what type of attitude or point you're trying to get across on any given day. For example, when Tony Soprano wears a suit, he has a good reason to wear it. Maybe there's business that needs to be taken care of that day; maybe there's a wedding or funeral or other special occasion. A tuxedo will always come in handy for your daughter's wedding or when you're being honored by some local boys and girls club for your generous donation.

Whatever you do, you want to avoid the Wall Street look at all costs. You are not a legitimate businessman, so why hassle yourself to look like one? Remember: avoid Wall Street; think Mulberry Street.

When you're not closing deals or having a very good reason to look sharp, feel free to wear your hangout clothes. What do you generally wear when you're just kicking around, with nowhere special to go? If you said jeans, pitch 'em. You never see a true wiseguy in jeans, though there is no hard-and-fast rule. Instead, replace your jeans with an assortment of comfortable slacks.

Joey Sausage demonstrates getting your point across to a wiseguy-in-training. Note the requisite pinkie ring and half-smoked cigar. (photo courtesy David Garofalo)

On top, don't wear golf shirts. Polo shirts are too damn WASPy and not what you're about at all. Take care to stock your wardrobe with a collection of oversized bowling shirts. Why oversized? For one, there's comfort. And there's always the chance that you will want to hide things in there—even an extra serving of linguine and clams—that no one else need know about.

Take It from Me . . .

Whatever you do, do not run out and get yourself a fedora. That look is out now and wearing one will only cause other mobsters to laugh at you.

Accessories Make the Made Man

Finishing touches are how you can make an individual statement, and here are some that should be addressed whenever you're getting dressed:

- *Sunglasses.* These are absolutely essential—not so much for protecting your eyes from the sun, but to protect them from giving your thoughts away and telling your enemies things you don't want them to know. (Sunglasses also come in handy for confusing witnesses and police artists.)

- *Necklace.* A gold cross on a chain, preferably blessed—by the pope himself, if you've really hit the big time.

- *Watches.* Have an assortment of top-name watches (Rolexes are best), the "hottest" timepieces money can buy—or would have bought had you actually paid for them . . .

- *Pinkie ring.* If you don't already know you're supposed to wear one of these, you have no business even getting this far in this book.

Please note: Always wear your wedding ring. It's important to remind people that you are, above all, a "family man."

Steal Only the Best: Cars for the Modern Mobster

A car is a status symbol for any man but, for a made man, it sends a message. A car screams volumes about your monetary success; the fancier, more-souped-up, more-tripped-out your car is, the more success you are having.

And let's face it: Any car that doesn't have enough trunk room to stash a body or stolen merchandise is not worth the sticker price. You don't want to have to whack someone and put him in the backseat. That's just embarrassing—although it could be a good ploy for the HOV lane. Unless you actually get pulled over, that is.

Throughout the years, certain standards have arisen for mobsters, regarding the cars they drive. For those averse to mammoth, Darth Vader–like SUVs like the Ford Explorer, the Cadillac *is* the classic wiseguy car. They never go out of style—and they're hard to wire for exploding devices, too.

In recent years, the Lexus has been making a pretty fair showing in mob circles. Its roomy interior satisfies basic needs of carting fenced goods—and not to mention driving all night to dispose of a body in the woods you don't want found (and that's when those GPS navigation systems come in handy, to locate those out-of-the-way spots perfect for a burial ground)—in sumptuous comfort.

And let's not forget the old reliable Lincoln Town Car. Yes, it is a "poor man's Cadillac," but it's good for the wiseguy on a budget, or one who has to moonlight as a car service driver to pull in some extra bucks.

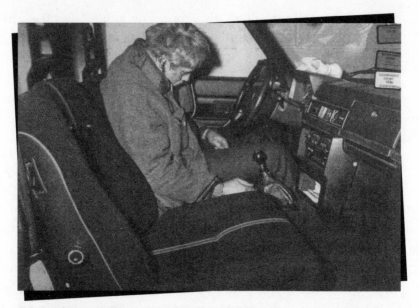

The late Bobby Bagels drove a Japanese car. When his crew took him for a ride, he got great mileage. (photo courtesy U.S. Attorney's Office, Eastern District of New York)

Then there are a whole group of cars a mobster would not want to be caught dead in the trunk of:

- The Honda Civic, Accord, the Toyota Camry or Corolla . . . in fact, no Japanese car is appropriate for a mobster to be driving around in. Let's take that a step further: All imports are out. Buy American. Always buy or "borrow" American. Support the people that support you. (Except when it comes to fashion, of course.)

- The VW beetle has never stricken fear or impressed anyone.

- The Volvo is a terrible car for a mobster. The Volvo is associated with soccer moms—soccer moms and baby seats. Certainly not anything that will stir up fear in the hearts of your enemies and underlings.

- Hyundai. No comment required.

- Mini Cooper. Forget the fact that it's as gay as a day in May. Where are you going to put a body in a goddamned Mini Cooper!?!

- The Chrysler PT Cruiser looks like an old-time gangster sedan but, again, it's all about size. If you must purchase one of these to get "into character," think of the PT Cruiser as a good training car, but steal something better when the opportunity presents itself.

In the simplest terms, any vehicle considered an "economy car" is out. As a rule, in cars and most anything else in the mobster lifestyle, bigger is always better. It's not like you're worried about mileage or the environment.

---

15 Songs You Need to Know to Be in the Mafia

1. "When Your Old Wedding Ring Was New" sung by Jimmy Roselli

2. "Mambo Italiano" sung by Rosemary Clooney

3. "Hey, Brother, Pour the Wine" sung by Dean Martin

4. "Arrivederci Roma" sung by Dean Martin

5. "Mama Get the Hammer (There's a Fly On Papa's Head)" sung by Lou Monte

6. "Rags to Riches" sung by Tony Bennett

7. "Speak Softly" sung by Al Martino

8. "That's Amore" sung by Dean Martin

9. "Pretend You Don't See Her" sung by Jerry Vale

(continued on next page)

---

10. "I Have but One Heart" sung by Vic Damone

11. "Eh, Cumpari" sung by Julius LaRosa

12. "Angelina" sung by Louis Prima

13. "Mona Lisa" sung by Nat King Cole

14. "Who's Sorry Now" sung by Connie Francis

15. "Papa Loves Mambo" sung by Perry Como

(You'll note that there's not a single Frank Sinatra title on this list. That's because you should already know Sinatra is a necessity without being told. If you didn't think of it, you're a fuckin' mook and should look for another line of work.)

Italian Food–Good or Bad, You Better Get Used to It

We all like lasagne and pepperoni pizza and sausage and peppers, but you can get that shit in a package of Hot Pockets. No, if you're gonna start your own mob—and do it right—you got to eat 100 percent Italian, like stuffed artichokes and fried calamari and veal Sorrentino. (So named for Angelo Sorrentino, who used to run a kick-ass joint up on Arthur Avenue.)

Also, you take your coffee black. Milk and sugar are for fags and losers. If your coffee goes down without scorching your vocal cords or blistering your colon, you need stronger coffee. And forget that Starbucks shit—six bucks for a coffee is an *infamia*, a sin. Your money is better spent paying tribute to yourself.

Remember in *The Godfather*, Louie's Restaurant in the Bronx, where Al Pacino goes to take a leak and grabs the gun taped to the toilet tank? He goes out and drills the drug dealer Solozzo and that corrupt Irish cop, McCluskey, two bullets each in the head. Apiece, just like Clemenza taught him.

This joint may not look fancy, but they make the best pizza in Brooklyn. Also, an unassuming joint like this makes a great hangout, provided there's a back room available for meetings. (photo courtesy Kevin Helmick)

When it comes to Italian food, *The Godfather* nails it. The first thing the waiter does in Louie's Restaurant is set down Italian bread and a platter of carrots, celery, and olives, what the Jews call a relish tray. Then he uncorks the Chianti. The following exchange says it all:

McCLUSKEY (Sterling Hayden): How's the Italian food in this joint?

SOLOZZO (Al Lettieri): Excellent. Try the veal, it's the best in the city.

McCluskey does, and it goes down a lot easier than those two bullets Pacino pumps into his head and throat, respectively. What's important to note is that McCluskey has the veal speared on the fork halfway to his mouth when he goes face-down into the antipasto.

The moral is, good veal is worth dying for.

The point I'm trying get across here is, food is very important in the mob. Any mook can eat at McDonalds or TGI Friday's. A real mafioso wouldn't be caught dead in one of those joints. No, you got to have a real honest-to-God Italian restaurant. And not just for the food—your Italian restaurant is where you'll be holding meetings and sit-downs and working out the day-to-day problems that naturally arise when you're running a criminal enterprise.

I mean what the hell—how's it going to look if you call a meeting with the head of a rival crime family in a Waffle House? You're going to have a serious credibility problem.

If you live in one of those rural small towns in the middle of nowhere and there's no good Italian joint, my advice is to either move to a place that does have one or, if you don't want to move, open one up yourself.

It's easier than you think. Buy everything on credit. It'll take six months to a year for your creditors to track you down, and by that time you've already torched the joint for the insurance (otherwise known as Jewish lightning).

And no matter how much you've had to eat, dessert is always mandatory. Treat yourself to a savory slice of tiramisu, or indulge in a traditional Italian pastry or cookie: sfogliatelle, cannoli, biscotti, regina cookies—plain and sesame. There's nothing like a sweet and a shot of espresso and a Sambuca to get that digestion to kick in.

Pasta Shapes and Their Correct Pronunciations

Watching a wiseguy not know how to order pasta is like watching a Frenchman who knows nothing about wine—it's just unforgivable. Call it pasta or call it macaroni, but every made man should know how to identify at least five pasta shapes. Here are the basics:

Basic

Spaghetti (spa-GEH-tee): If you don't know what this is, you're just a *gavone.*

Linguine (lin-GUEE-nee): As above, except these guys are skinnier.

Ravioli (rav-YOH-lee): Even Chef Boyardee knows when you take some pasta, stuff it with cheese or meat, and fold it over, it's called ravioli.

A Bit More Advanced

Farfalle (far-FALL-eh): Known as "bowties" and "butterflies"—but if you order "butterflies" in front of your crew, be prepared to get whacked for being light in your designer loafers.

Fettuccine (fett-u-CHEE-nee): Long, flat noodles usually served with Alfredo sauce.

Gnocchi (NO-key): Potato dumplings that pass as pasta—sort of like Tater Tots dipped in cement.

Rigatoni (rig-a-TONE-ee): Large tube-shaped pasta most often served "alla vodka."

Impress Your Friends!

Acini pepe (a-CHEE-nee PEH-pey): These beady guys look like barley, and are used mostly in soups.

Conchiglie (con-KEEL-yay): Pasta shells. (Conchiglioni are the large shells you fill with ricotta for stuffed shells.)

Gigli (JI-glee): This pasta is especially delicious with chunky meat sauces, but be sure to order it with the Italian name. (It translates into English as "lilies"—and do you really want your crew to know you're eating flowers?)

Trenette (tre-NET-tay): Looks like linguine—but it's longer and hollow. Best as a side dish.

Do Wiseguys Cook?

In a word, yes, but not a lot. A basic understanding of pastas and sauces never hurt anyone, but that doesn't mean you have to actually make any of them.

Most of the cooking in the mobster milieu falls to the wife, though every boss should have at least one signature dish he can make for his crew. It doesn't have to be fancy, unless you want it to be. But whether it's osso buco or plain old linguine and clams, decide what that meal should be and really work at making it the best you and your men have ever had. They'll really appreciate the effort you put into it.

Of course, your wife needs to know the whole gamut of Italian cooking, and must be trained to whip up a seven-course meal on a moment's notice. It's about respect. When you roll in with some of your crew at three in the morning after a rough night of drinking, gambling, whoring, or stuffing body parts into a wood chipper, she should be ready to whip up a platter of spaghetti and sausage and eggs and peppers.

If your wife can't cook, you may have to consider replacing her. I'm sorry to say this, but cooking is one of the most important jobs a Mafia wife has; it's truly not negotiable, a deal-breaker.

Of course, there are alternatives to actually replacing her. You can insist. As a mob boss, one of your most important skills is the ability to insist—and make people bend to your will. And seriously, if you can't even wear down your own wife, what good are you gonna be on the street? Think about it.

Maybe it's not that your wife won't cook, but that she can't. Oh, the poor thing. She so wants to please her man but when it comes to wielding spatulas and wooden spoons, she's just all thumbs.

Yeah. I don't buy that crap and neither should you. If she can dial a phone for takeout, she can knead bread dough, crank a pasta maker, even chop tomatoes.

Every woman can cook. If your wife is pretending to be deficient in this arena—maybe she needs a little old-fashioned encouragement. Show her that there's a whole TV channel out there ready to teach her. If that doesn't work, bring your nagging mother over for a week or two to stick her nose into everything your wife does, from cleaning the bathrooms to disciplining the kids. Watch how fast wifey learns to cook.

If your wife still refuses to cook after all the help you give her, you may have to take the most drastic measure of all: cut off the money tap so she can't shop. You'll show her who's boss faster than a fart in a backdraft. . .

> *"I asked my wife, where do you wanna go for our anniversary? She said, 'Take me some place I've never been to.' I said, 'Try the kitchen.'"*
>
> — Henny Youngman, *GoodFellas* (1990)

Wives aside, it's always smart to have one guy in your crew who can cook. You never know when you're gonna have to "go to the mattresses" and hole up for weeks at a time. It's bad enough sleeping on smelly mattresses in drab, unfurnished apartments—the least you can expect is a decent meal.

Talk the Talk, Part 1

You can't be a mobster if you can't speak like one. Here's a list of preliminary terms to get you started.

Omertà: This is the sacred code of silence sworn when joining a family, and it extends throughout the Mafia community. If you break Omertà, you are a rat and you will be killed.

(continued on next page)

Friend of mine: Someone who isn't in your particular family, but who's still highly trusted by members of your family.

Friend of ours: When you're walking down the street with one of your mob buddies, and you run into another made man that he knows and you don't, this is how he will introduce you to each other.

Oobatz: In a word, crazy. But not just your average nut: It's the kind of crazy that knows no limits to malice and mayhem (see Joseph Gallo, page 21).

Closing Thoughts

Becoming a mobster is a very serious decision, and one that cannot be made lightly. As we'll show you time and again in this book, the chances of enjoying your retirement and living to a ripe old age, giving yourself time to deplete the fortune that you amass for yourself and your family, are very rare.

Your rise to the top will be filled with obstacles and hurdles. And when you finally get there, you may only get a quick peek of the good life. No one gets to stay. Plan to be pushed, thrown, kicked, arrested, or whacked right off the top. But, hey, at least you can say you were there. As John Gotti once said: "I'd rather be a lion for a day than a sheep for a lifetime."

As a mobster, there really are only three ways your story will end: (1) you'll serve an interminable jail sentence, (2) you'll get whacked (the most common scenario), or (3) you will end up in the Witness Protection Program, which is like death, only more bleak because God knows where you're gonna get relocated—and if a guy can even get a decent calzone there. Then again, another way to look at it is as government-financed Social Security for mobsters. The government's supporting wiseguys for the rest of their lives in crime-free communities—and guys who never paid a dollar of taxes in their entire career, to boot! Who's laughing now?

So knowing all this, do you still want it? Of course you do, you crazy SOB. Now let's get started.

CHAPTER 3

Getting Started

or,

Welcome to the Age of Entitlement

*When I introduce you, I'm gonna say, "This is a
friend of mine." That means you're a connected guy.
Now if I said instead, "This is a friend of ours,"
that would mean you're a made guy. Capisce?*
—Benjamin "Lefty" Ruggiero (Al Pacino), *Donnie Brasco* (1997)

SURE, YOU HAVE A LOVE OF EXPENSIVE CLOTHES AND JEWELRY, OF FAST
cars and faster women. And yes, maybe you do wake up nights
planning what you'll do with all that tax-free cash. And when
you do finally get to sleep, you periodically whack people in
your dreams. But do you really have what it takes to make the
big time?

It's one thing to say that you want to become a mobster.
But if you don't act on it, and spend your life stuck at your
dead-end job dreaming and scheming, we don't want you.
We're all for visionaries, but being a mobster requires an action plan.

What it all comes down to is that you gotta want it, and
then some. You have to be willing to push anyone who stands

in your way out of the way, even if that person happens to be your white-haired old walker-bound aunt or your own cousins.

Yes, there are many pros to this lifestyle, and the cons (incarceration, early death) may be too much for some. But if you're the type who's not going to let a little thing like a dirt nap get in the way, you might be just what we're looking for. Ask yourself this:

- Do you want it as bad as you wanted that new bike on Christmas morning when you were a kid?

- Are you focused and disciplined?

- Are you in control of that pain-in-the-ass little nuisance people call a conscience? Because if not, it's going to get in the way.

- A mobster never takes a day off. Are you willing to make a twenty-four-hours-a-day, seven-days-a-week commitment to it, even if it pisses off your wife (which it will)?

- Are you emotionally prepared to use a cattle prod to your oldest and dearest friend if you suspect him of talking to the feds?

Remember, you can't just wake up one morning and decide to be something else. Once you take the first step, there's no turning back.

In this chapter, you will:

- Test your mobster mettle and see if you really have what it takes to become a crime boss

- Learn the steps you need to take to get your venture off the ground

- Explore the many options available to you to keep your new business running and thriving

Do You Have What It Takes?

How many of these attributes apply to you?

	Yes	No	Maybe
Brains and cunning	❏	❏	❏
Ice water in your veins	❏	❏	❏
Eyes in the back, side, and top of your head	❏	❏	❏
Psychic ability	❏	❏	❏
Killing instincts of a cheetah	❏	❏	❏
Survival instincts of a cockroach	❏	❏	❏
Complete and utter fearlessness (Note: It's not a compliment if you're not smart enough to be afraid)	❏	❏	❏
An ability to hear everything said about you—even in other states	❏	❏	❏
A complete disregard for other people's property	❏	❏	❏
A complete disregard for feelings not your own	❏	❏	❏
A complete disregard for authority	❏	❏	❏

(continued on next page)

	Yes	No	Maybe
A complete disregard for human life (Can you enjoy a full meal and a good night's sleep after a hit?)	❏	❏	❏
A community to harass (You can't be a mobster in isolation.)	❏	❏	❏

What You Need to Succeed

If you answered yes to most of those questions, you're probably a strong contender for becoming a big-time mafioso. But
it's not enough to have what it takes—or even to look good in
a pinkie ring. You need strength, my friend. The strength to wear
ten pounds of gold on any given day or night. You need thick
skin and bulletproof hair.

As a crime boss, you're not getting into the business to make
friends. It's all about making money, at any cost. The Mafia is
not a popularity contest and you're not running for homecoming
queen. You need to rule with an iron fist, and to be seen as someone who is unapproachable—even to your own wife, children, or
mother. You have to be willing to make unpopular decisions
during hard times, even if that means killing your best friend
for the good of all.

Not that you'll really have friends. That's like saying Attila
the Hun had friends. No. What you need is more along the lines
of a group of worshippers, who will do anything for you because
they're scared to death of you. And you really have to take advantage of that. True, you have to be diplomatic enough that they
don't revolt against you, and charismatic enough that they might
actually enjoy doing your bidding. And you have to make them
feel that they're getting at least something out of it. Toss them

To run a successful mob crew, you need scary-looking guys like this with names like Cheech and Mr. Tony. (photo courtesy U.S. Attorney's Office, Eastern District of New York)

a bone every now and then. Remember: You always want to keep your men fed, but never full.

As a mob boss, your raison d'etre is to motivate others to kill and steal and lie and cheat for you. Anybody can commit a crime for himself, but only a mob boss can get hundreds to do it for him.

Take It from Me . . .

It doesn't hurt to have a couple of legendary stories—truth or bullshit—that detail your incredible conquests involving women, bloodshed, big scores (e.g., heists), and even jail terms—anything to brag about. Your crew should think of you as Superman—but without anything like kryptonite holding you back.

Pulling It All Together

Like any professional, a mobster has basic needs. How you satisfy these will demonstrate your strength and staying power as a leader. If you have siblings—recruit them. If you have kids, even better. Bring them on board! If you don't have kids, make them. Now. And try and make only sons, if you can help it. You need blood relatives on board. You also need:

- A right-hand guy
- And a left-hand guy to keep an eye on the right-hand guy
- And another guy to watch over both of them
- A good tailor. Italian whenever possible
- A lawyer with a proven record of success in your chosen field—a good deal maker
- An accountant who won't get greedy
- A driver
- Girlfriends—aside from wife
- Friends in law enforcement—legitimate high places/offices, such as politicians, etc.
- The best hangouts but not fucking Starbucks
- An arsenal of grandma's recipes
- The ability to know what to do when the shit hits the fan. Be cool in a crisis. Have a poker face. Know when to kill. Know when to keep your head down. Know when *not* to kill. Know when to hold 'em; know when to fold 'em. Know when to fish and when to cut bait and any other cliches I forgot.
- The ability to deliver cryptic, undecipherable messages over a cell phone
- Lip-reading skills
- Multiple addresses, none of them real if possible
- Cash stashes, because no wise guy bothers with a bank, unless it's to rob it. *And you never want anyone to ever know how much you really have.*

Networking

I told you before and I'll tell you again: A mob boss is not an island. If the people in your community are not aware of you, and don't know they're supposed to be afraid of you, you may as well be the mailman or the paperboy.

As in any entrepreneurial venture, networking is the core of your business success. To that end, you need to focus on and develop your brand. It's the same for any business: branding is everything.

Your nickname goes a long way in presenting your brand to the world (which is why you should choose your own—and make it a good one), but your actions will speak louder than any words. If you call yourself "the Crusher," be sure and have at the ready a few examples of people and places you have actually crushed—factual or fictional. (It's not like anyone's actually going to check these references, which is one of the definite perks of not being legit!)

Your underlings can go a long way in spreading your message. Once you initiate them, and dazzle them with the story of you, give them the charge of enforcing your legend. It will make them feel special, like they're part of the effort, and you get the added benefit of more exposure for you without having to do the legwork yourself.

Also beneficial to you will be your marks, or the people you choose to do business with you. Be very attentive to the details of your first "partnership." Your new partner, a.k.a. the guy whose delivery truck you have just hijacked, should feel confident in making the choice to let you "help" his operation, and that there simply was no better choice for him in terms of taking on a new partner. He should feel this strongly enough that he will tell his distributors, clients, customers, and other colleagues all about how, well, "professional" you are, and be able to recommend you to his associates without hesitation.

Referrals are a beautiful way to grow a business, but only through building a strong network will you ever be able to enjoy these kinds of rewards.

Taking Over an Existing Family—or Starting Your Own?

For better or worse, the Mafia isn't what it used to be in terms of scope and might. But don't worry about that: this can be a very good thing for you.

Think about it. On the one hand, there may not be as much competition as you would have faced years ago; and on the other, you may just be able to resuscitate a dying industry and become a hero of future mob lore for generations to come!

Historically, there have been twenty-six Mafia families and, in its heyday, there were about three thousand members of Cosa Nostra across the United States. Currently, there are less than ten families, and ensuing generations are becoming less and less interested in following in their forefathers' felonious footsteps.

This could be a great opportunity for you! With the proper legwork, you might stumble across one of these families looking for a real go-getter to lead them and, without a lot of interference, you can slip right in to the role of don, an established operation up and running and cutting out all that startup aggravation!

As we'll get into later in this chapter, a little competition can be a very healthy thing, but if you face too much, chances are pretty good you'll find yourself facedown in a bowl of linguine and red sauce—that used to be white. *Capisce?*

Take It from Me . . .

As a successful mobster, you'll have to be loved, liked, and feared all at the same time. Yes, it's an unusual combination, but just think of the way you feel about your mother.

Location! Location! Location!

These days, with the global economy expanding like crazy, it's no longer necessary to conduct your mob business in one of the major cities. Nowadays, you can enjoy all the charm and comforts of your hometown, without having to commute—and you can corrupt the crap out of it!

Your operation will be run out of several places, depending on the task at hand for any given day. There's your home office, which is good for shredding paper trails. Next, there's your social club, a great place for networking and an excellent venue for dealing with current business when you want your "partners" to pay you a visit.

Finally, there's the core of your business: the streets where you live. Here are all the small businesses you will happily and freely embezzle from, as well as hookers, drug czars, you name it. It's all there for the taking!

You knew being a mobster had a lot of perks. Here's one you may not have considered: exercise. Mobsters do not go to gyms, but working the streets can keep you fit. Truly, what better way could there be to work off last night's pasta than with a little strength-building, cardio-challenging, body-and-mind flexibility training (at least in a moral sense) from bullying and violence.

Your "Business Plan"

Every successful legitimate business needs something called a "business plan" if it's going to flourish, and your Mafia operation is no exception.

Whereas some businesses will need to spell out all effort and intent for possible investors, you need only concentrate on your own personal goals: it's not like you're going after any bank funding (see "Scaring Up Capital," page 67)—unless you're looking to knock one over, naturally.

In fact, one of the great things about starting a Mafia family is that you don't need a lot, or really any, capital to get it off the ground. Look back to chapter 1. Most of the truly successful Mafia heroes started out as poor urchins and gutter-snipes who scratched and bit and killed their way to the top.

Creating a Business Plan for Your Mob Venture

Yes, it's a good idea to have a business plan in place but, once you do, it is of the utmost importance that you burn the elements into your brain—and then actually *burn* the plan, or destroy it in another way that it can't be recovered to implicate you in a court of law. Opt for the old standards of pen or pencil and paper. Even if you delete the file on your computer, you can bet the feds have some mamby-assed computer geek loser who can crack open your hard drive and send you serving hard time. Here are the elements you should be focusing on:

The Concept. If you want to get anywhere with your Mafia venture, you need to have a fully thought-out concept in place, one that will help you establish your goals as clearly as possible and help you focus your efforts. Think about your mission; what kinds of services will you provide that sets you apart from the other guy?

For example: Let's say the greedhead politicians in your state decide to raise the taxes on a pack of cigarettes by fifty cents or even a dollar. (Don't laugh—they did just this in New York City.) Sure, the politicians say it's for your own good: maybe you'll quit smoking when you're looking at six or seven dollars a pack. We all know politicians are full of shit—hell, all that lotto money was supposed to pay for improving schools and the educational system in America. Yet, billions of dollars later, we're still spitting out a generation of illiterates from our schools with nary an improvement from the government.

Yet the smoker's loss is your gain—there's a need now for cheap coffin nails. Start hijacking truckloads of Marlboros and Lucky Strikes. Then distribute them to the local convenience stores for forty cents on the dollar.

The Objective. With your concept fully in place, you can really hone in on what you want to achieve. What are your expectations in terms of profits and, especially important for a mob boss, scope of power? Try and be as specific as possible. Instead of saying: "I want to corner the market on mob-related activities," focus your thinking to make it something you can really quantify, and you'll be able to achieve it much more quickly.

Market Analysis. Yes, the competition has been dwindling in recent years, but you can't make the mistake of ignoring it altogether. It still exists, and it's there, pistol cocked, waiting to take you down.

Your best bet for starting out, however, is to zero in on your direct competition. It's going to take some time for you to be up to par with the Gottis and Gambinos of the world; you may want to focus your energy first on the action going on in your own neighborhood. What? You think you're the only one in your subdivision to think this up? It's that kind of thinking that's going to knock you out of the running before you corner your first racket. See what the competition is doing and mold your plan around improving on it.

Actual Marketing. You're only going to be as effective as your wrath—and what people know of it. If they don't know you're lurking in the shadows, how will they ever know they're supposed to give you money and favors in exchange for your protection?

Organization and People. We're going to get more into this later, but before you embark on staffing your operation, you should think long and hard on who's going to be out there representing you—and filling the cement shoes of your enemies. Start thinking about all the various positions that need to be filled—consigliere, enforcer, baboo (because every family needs one)—and concentrate on who should be making up your inner circle.

Financial Projections. Basically, this is about monitoring cash flow: your cash in (and potential sources), your cash out (where your money might go, be it jewelry for your wife or goomar, a bribe for your favorite judge, et cetera), and timing, which is everything, right? Be realistic about when cash will flow in and out of your stash, so you always have a stack of clipped hundreds available for tipping and general showing off.

Ownership. It's all yours, baby. In case you needed any reminding.

Wiseguys in the Mainstream

Scarface, which was released in 1932 and again in 1983, is based on the life of Al Capone.

Scaring Up Capital

I know you don't believe this, but starting a Mafia organization as compared to another kind of business is actually cheap. So the only capital you really need to focus on is human: you, your underlings, and how much you're able to scare others into handing over money, property, power, or what-have-you.

When it comes to mob money, it's always a question of robbing both Peter and Paul—to pay yourself. We'll get more into this when we examine rackets and other business opportunities a bit later.

Take It from Me . . .
True mob bosses get everything "on the broch." If you're not enjoying services and goods "on the broch," it's time to employ some serious scare tactics.

Publicity

As we discussed earlier (or rather, as I discussed earlier—you don't know ugatz; if you did, you wouldn't be reading this), publicity in the Mafia can be very dangerous. Sure, you love how people kiss your ass and satisfy your every whim because they either fear you or are strongly attracted to the power you radiate.

However, too much publicity—like getting on the local news or on the front page of the newspapers—will attract the attention of all the wrong people, such as the cops and the feds. It's always better to keep the lowest profile possible. Learn from the mistakes made by the likes of Lucky Luciano and John Gotti. They loved the attention and the media exposure. And it was their downfall. Luciano was deported and Gotti died in prison.

Some Things You Never Have to Worry About

Some (legitimate) business owners have hassles that prevent them from ever turning a profit or cause them to work all the time, never enjoying the fruits of their labor. Luckily, you are not legit, so there are many things you'll never have to worry about, such as:

A Web Site. Seriously, how vain can you possibly be. And what would you have there? Photos of your goomars? Your contact information? A chat room? Fuggedabouddit! If you're worth your weight in malice, some geek is going to post something about you soon enough, anyway. You'll at least end up on Wikipedia.com.

Inventory and Overhead. These are the suckers' trappings. The only people who need to worry about these kinds of things are the marks you plan to hit. After all, isn't one of the simplest joys of being a mobster living at the expense of others?

Paying Taxes. Again, a sucker's bet. Remember: You're running a cash and kill business, and it's none of Fat Sam's business how much you're raking in.

Pesky, Expensive Employee Perks. Good news! As a mob boss, you're simply not obligated to do things for your staff that legit businessmen are. Health insurance? Fuggedabouddit! Pensions,

401(k)s, or other retirement plans? The only way one retires from this business is on a beach vacation—in other words, washing up on the banks of a nearby river. And paid time off? You're not paying your men to sit around on their asses, and that's it. Keep in mind that this doesn't mean you have to be chintzy with your staff. There are plenty of perks you can offer underlings, many of which can also benefit you. But more about this later.

Take It from Me . . .
Every mob boss has one thing in common: Extremely good luck. At least for a little while, anyway. Soon enough, someone's going to get greedy and turn on you—whether that means ratting you out, whacking you, or otherwise ruining you. So if you get to the top, you'd better be sure to enjoy it while you can . . . Any day above ground is a good one.

Closing Thoughts

As much as this handbook will provide you with invaluable information to get you started in your career, success in gangland depends almost 100 percent on luck. Even if you take this book as a bible and follow every instruction to the letter, without good luck, you're as good as whacked. There's one thing you must never forget: stray bullets hit mobsters.

Your reign can go on as long as a decade or as short as a power lunch. No one knows how many months are in your destiny. So make it your top priority and your career mission to live it up each and every day. Because one day, you will get whacked, and chances are fairly good that you will not see it coming.

CHAPTER 4

The Players

or,

A Family Affair

MICHAEL CORLEONE (Al Pacino): **Do you still fear me,
Kay?**
KAY CORLEONE (Diane Keaton): **I don't fear you,
Michael, I just dread you.**
—*The Godfather Part III*

THE ONLY *I* IN THE TEAM YOU'RE GOING TO BE ASSEMBLING IS THE
M and the *E*. But you can't run your operation without a wide
range of other talent. Here's where personnel selection is all
important.

You want associates who are as greedy as you are but
nowhere near as smart. If they're too smart, why should they
work for you? They'll go off and start their own gangs. You
might even wind up working for them. And then you're right
back where you started. Remember, the real fun in this business comes from being the boss.

In this chapter, you will learn:

- The various positions of the Mafia hierarchy—and how
  to fill those slots

- The means to keep your "family" loyal

- How to keep "problem employees" under control

> ### *Take It from Me ...*
> A high school dropout with a long criminal history of violence, assault, armed robbery, and attempted murder, should rank high on your list of potential hires.

Who's Who in a Mafia Family?

In traditional Mafia families, the highest positions could only be filled by 100 percent Italians. Where you live, it's possible you may not even know any Italians, and that's fine; for your family, you set the rules.

When pulling your team together, use the term *crew*. Not only is this correct, it will also make your people feel like they're part of a forward-moving mass, like a rowing crew.

The Italian thing aside, however, you must put careful thought into choosing your underlings. After all, these are the people who will be representing you in the outside world as they do your bidding, and you want to make sure they are properly assigned to appropriate roles.

Typical families include a boss, an underboss, and capos—each with his own crew made up of a team of soldiers who perform most of the dirty work.

Boss

It should go without saying that this is the role you want for yourself, and the only role you should be considering.

Here's the kind of guy you want for your underboss. Don't let the kind face fool you: this guy is a master at damage control—first cause the damage, then control it. (photo courtesy Bartolo Raffaele)

As the head of the family, you'll be known as the "don" or "godfather," and you'll be in control of everyone. As late as the 1950s, entire families would get together to vote on who the next boss would be, but that was pure chaos. Another alternative was that the boss would be chosen by a vote from the capos. If there was ever a tie, the underboss would decide the winner.

This is all well and good, but it should in no way apply to you. Remember, you're starting this operation from scratch; you don't need to get bogged down in all these senseless details.

As boss, as you can well imagine, you will enjoy many perks, such as a cut of every operation taken on by every member of your family. You'll also have the love, respect, fear, dread, and more of everyone underneath you. Ah, it's good to be king!

Underboss

You better think long and hard about who your underboss is going to be, because not only will he be second-in-command to you, he'll also be in charge of all the capos. He's also first in line for your job should you get ill or incarcerated—or killed.

The underboss should be someone who's almost qualified to be the boss but just misses the mark. It's a role to be filled by someone who's good enough to run things when you're not there, but not strong enough to take over.

If you're lucky enough to find someone with the right qualifications who has the same blood as you, or is intimately related to someone who shares blood with you, bend down and kiss the ground. It's a lot easier to keep tabs on your sister's husband than it is to handle some guy who isn't actually family.

Of course, you may not have a sister or brother. So who are some people you could consider to fill this essential role?

An underboss is essentially an administrator, so he might be the manager of a Target or some other store manager who's used to "moving herds." If you don't already have someone like this in your immediate social circle, scout the local Target, Wal-Mart, even Kmart, and raid the managerial hierarchy. Complain a lot and ask to "see the manager" as often as possible. Make your complaints as inane as you possibly can. You really want to test this guy's mettle—you want to see how far you can push him before he snaps. If he snaps at you or otherwise disrespects you, he's out. If he continues to kiss your ass, offers you free stuff, takes all your gripes and insults with a subversive smile (the mouth smiles, yes, but you can see in his eyes that he'd like to knock your lights out), take the guy out for a beer and offer him the job!

Consigliere

A consigliere is your adviser, your consultant, your coach. He is a crucial member of a Mafia family. An "outsider" on the inside, the only thing he stands to gain is keeping his position, and therefore, ensuring your success. He can't take over

A good consigliere is an absolute must for any successful mob boss. He must possess a keen intellect, diplomacy, a thorough knowledge and understanding of the law, and an ability to kill people. (photo courtesy U.S. Attorney's Office, Eastern District of New York)

because he's not family, but is it not true that sometimes your closest allies are not related to you?

Even though you are not relations, your consigliere holds a powerful position in your family. Without him, everything could go to shit.

The person you choose as consigliere should like to keep a low profile, but has to be someone who can be trusted. No loudmouths. He should be a respected member of the community or someone who could be perceived as respectable, because you will be relying on him to get in touch with and develop solid relationships with judges, politicians, and other powerful folks. He should belong to a country club and should be able to swing a golf club—good enough that he can use golf outings with these powerful folks as platforms for persuasion, but not so good that he'd ever beat them—with a golf club, that is.

The consigliere does damage control within and outside the family. He mediates disputes among family members as well as with other families, and helps keep the family looking legit.

All of this considered, your consigliere should be your smartest friend. If you live in the East, consider a lawyer. On the West Coast, a yoga instructor makes a fine choice. In the Midwest, a high school guidance counselor may be your best—and only—bet.

Essentially, you have to go with your gut. Does your friend seem to have your best interests at heart? Can he keep a secret? The choice, of course, is yours. But choose wisely. Remember: This person will know more about your business affairs than your wife and children, and your accountant (naturally).

Capo

Also known as a "captain," a capo in charge of a crew of soldiers, the guys who essentially do all the dirty work in the Mafia family—but we'll get more into that in a little bit.

When introducing capos into your family, look either at people who are assistant managers of large operations or to independent business owners of tanning parlors, hair salons, tuxedo rentals, local delis, that kind of thing.

These kinds of people know how to keep their small slice of the pie from getting eaten. They have a perfect middle-management sensibility, and usually know their place. For the most part, you can be assured if you added one of these types into your pool of capos, he'd get the job done and wouldn't necessarily strive for your position.

A good capo knows how to take all the credit and none of the blame. When his underlings make a big score, he'll be called innovative, successful, et cetera. When he screws up, he'll be forced to deny authorizing any of the mess.

Capos should be people who are happy with a small situation of power, because to them, whatever power that is is like an empire to them. And they will treat their underlings with the same mentality. This is actually a great thing for you. After all, the CEO should not be worried about the activities and shenanigans of the mailroom guys and secretaries; a good capo will have it covered.

Joey Sausage is the perfect capo—he doesn't take shit from his crew and provides the kind of strategic leadership necessary to manage a bunch of violent *gavones*. (photo courtesy David Garofalo)

Soldiers

Soldier is one of the lowest rungs in the hierarchy, and one some wiseguys will never get past. This is because a soldier has a small-time mentality, and they are usually very happy toiling away at whatever task has been handed to them. They are the worker bees, and are all delighted to be working to please the queen or, in this case, the king. That's you.

They will never go against the hive, nor will they let anyone on the outside infiltrate it. When someone threatens the existence of the hive, the soldiers sting. They also keep the hive running. They go out to get the pollen to make the honey, which rhymes with money, which is what they're going out into the world to collect for you. From flower to flower. From store to store, warehouse to warehouse, dock to dock, and so on.

> ### *Take It from Me . . .*
> A real mobster never pays full price for anything. If someone ever asks you to pay full price, consider yourself insulted and act accordingly. Start with a subtle, increasingly irritated tirade of "Do you know who I am? Do you know what I do?" If that doesn't work, call your underboss to call one of your capos to call one of his soldiers to "enforce" the point more clearly.

Alive in the Hive

This point cannot be made too many times: Your crew is essential to your operation. No mob boss is an island, especially when it comes to the work that needs to be done.

Remember, as a boss, you never give your enforcers direct orders. Oh, no. When you want something "taken care of," you

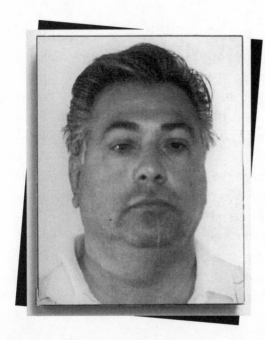

This is Richie Shellackhead. He got that nickname for having the thickest skull in the mob. (photo courtesy U.S. Attorney's Office, Eastern District of New York)

tell your underboss, who then tells a capo, who then assigns the job to a soldier, who gets it done. This is a time-tested way of doing things that will almost always ensure you keep out of the slammer should one of your underlings get caught in the act.

Wiseguys in the Mainstream

Jerry Orbach played a character based on Joe Gallo in *The Gang That Couldn't Shoot Straight* (1971).

Initiation

The traditional Mafia initiation ceremony has involved a certain amount of humiliation, a tiny amount of bloodshed, then smearing that blood on a picture of a saint, and a sacred pledge of loyalty, taken as the bloodied image was burned and the ashes scattered.

For your purposes, you don't have to go through all of this rigmarole. Modify the initiation ceremony into your family as you see fit.

Chances are pretty good that if you're reading this book, you're not Italian. Let's face it, if you were, you'd already have a pretty good inkling of how to get an operation like this off the ground. It's in your blood; the blueprints are imprinted on your DNA.

So you don't have to do everything the Italian way. You can instead create your own unique variation to the initiation ceremony. Just keep in mind that it's of the utmost importance that you think things through before you lay the cement on the ritual. Once it's dry, it's yours forever. For that reason, you want to take great care to formulate something you'll really be proud of and won't get sick of—something not trendy. You want a classic: a ceremony that will still resonate fifty, even a hundred, years from now.

Here's an example of a ceremony that someone who's forming his own family in Cheyenne, Wyoming, performed. For the
purposes of anonymity, this family shall remain nameless.

Each new inductee was required to wear a thousand-dollar
suit, two grams of yellow gold jewelry, and 1.5 ounces of cologne
to the ceremony.

Each was asked to eat one pound of pasta cooked al dente,
with homemade *marinara fetto di pomodoro* sauce.

Each inductee was instructed to deliver his own monologue,
from memory, from one of the *Godfather* films.

Each was then asked to pledge his allegiance to the family,
promising to try to do his best not to get caught. No blood-
letting or religious symbol was used, but there was a secret olive
oil ceremony—the details of which were not disclosed to us.

If you're thinking these are a bunch of old farts hanging out doing
nothing, think again. This is an actual mob crew from Brooklyn
discussing their big score—maybe knocking over a warehouse in
Queens or opening a chop shop for stolen cars. (*From left to right*)
Andy Cigars, Johnny Kneecaps, Billy the Bug, Big Frankie, Sal the Wop,
Jackie Rolex, and Petey Dark Eyes. (photo courtesy Andrew
Lombardozzi)

Again, this was the way one boss of a Wyoming crime family decided to go about his business. You may consider going the old route, or even making up your own olive oil ceremony. You might even consider looking to your local chapter of Boy Scouts and see how they do it.

Whatever you decide, just remember to give it a lot of thought. The last thing you want is a ceremony that's so "out there," you'll get raided and arrested before you even make your first dirty dollar!

Film and TV Mobsters, Part 2

Here are some more great examples of when mob life should—or shouldn't—imitate life.

The Sopranos

Your family can give you more problems than your crime family, so make sure you don't bite off more than you can chew when deciding how big your family should be. And this is the main reason mobsters have goomars. Think about it: When was the only time Tony was truly happy? When he was fucking someone who wasn't his wife. There's that—and also try to avoid New Jersey at all costs.

The Godfather Parts I, II, and III

You can pick your friends but you can't pick your relatives. Family comes first, second, third. Never go against the family, or you will pay dearly. Also, keep your friends close and your enemies closer. And potential traitors? Keep them closest of all.

Donnie Brasco

You have no friends and whatever friends you do think you have will eventually kill you. This movie beautifully reinforces the two inevitable endings of your career—death or jail. Remember: There were more survivors from the *Titanic* and other epic disasters as there are surviving mobsters.

Motivational Tactics

Just as in any business, if morale is down, productivity will slide. To that end, you want to keep your staff happy. True, some of the drudgery of their everyday existence is enough to make them want to put bullets through their own heads, but you must always remind them of the perks they are able to enjoy only because they are your underlings.

Just don't overdo it. Remember: Always keep your employees fed, but not full. Here are some prime carrots or employee incentives you can wave in front of their faces when defection or even mutiny seems imminent:

- *Discounts.* On everything from houses to cars, right on down to air travel, jewelry, even a quart of milk.

- *Unlimited access.* Your staff will never need to make reservations at any restaurant ever, and will have access to any event in town. It's all about access: to sporting events, theater, private parties, and more.

- *Free upgrades.* Whether it's fashion or a move to the first-class cabin in an airplane, because they are affiliated with you, they get the royal treatment.

- *The best doctors.* Having these medicine men scurrying around at your whim is one of the many reasons health insurance will never be an issue with your staff. That, and that most don't live long enough to get sick.

- *The scraps that fall off your table.* This could be stolen goods, girlfriends you don't want anymore, even mob groupies. Seconds are never considered "sloppy" when they come from the boss!

- *Life ensurance.* When they're in with you, they, and their friends and family members, will live and enjoy a certain level of protection. Of course, if they fall out of favor with you and the family, or one of their kids fucks up, or one of their wives mouths off, this policy will be subject to immediate revocation.

Talk the Talk, Part 2

Baboo: An underling considered to be useless. Every mob family needs one of these. Just make sure it's not you. The average term-of-service for a baboo could be weeks; it's seldom years. But there will always be a replacement waiting in the wings.

Broken: Essentially, this means getting demoted. Just like in any organization, a demotion is never pretty, and could lead to discord and your death. So keep a watchful eye on your broken staff. The best way to "clock" (see below) an especially volatile person is to have him safely stashed six feet underground or even under mounds of rotting trash at the local dump.

Clock: To keep a person—whether he's a part of your family, an associate, a friend in a high place, a potential threat to the "hive"—under surveillance.

Make: To identify; also, to induct as a member of the Mafia

Man of respect: This is you, your underboss, and your consigliere. It's a term bestowed only upon senior management.

Evaluating Performance

How well is your organization working? We'll, just as in any company, it all comes down to your staff. Are your people working tirelessly and selflessly to do all they can to make you a rich and powerful man? Ask yourself:

- How much money are your people bringing in?
- What's the profit margin—in other words, how much are they bringing in as compared to how much it's costing you to keep them around?

- Are they keeping their mouths shut?

- Are they keeping a low profile?

- Are they loyal? Here's a great test to find out: Tell each of your guys one thing, and see which bit of information gets back to you first within a ninety-day period.

- Are they paying proper tributes to you—for Christmas, your birthday, or random acts of giving to you, just to "say they care."

- How fat is the envelope (the *abusta*) they gave for your daughter's wedding?

To track growth and potential of each of your "employees" and to ensure they aren't slacking off, be sure to evaluate performance at least twice a year—and best if you can look at performance monthly, or even weekly. If they are not living up to your standards, disciplinary action may be in order.

Managing "Problem Employees"

When it comes to managing your staff and keeping them in line, there is no paperwork. It's not like you have warning slips that you file away, and once they accumulate a certain amount, disciplinary action is in order.

The easiest way to discipline your underlings is through the wallet. When people get out of line, you tighten the purse strings. When that doesn't work, a good backroom beating, tongue lashing, humiliation in front of the crew, à la Tony Soprano, will generally do the trick. In fact, for a mobster, there is no greater punishment than public humiliation. Something to keep in mind if you're watching your budget and don't want to overspend on bullets.

Wiseguys in the Mainstream

Once Upon a Time in America's David "Noodles"
Aaronson (Robert De Niro) is based on Meyer Lansky.

Having Your Very Own Strip Joint

Any mobster worth his weight in sopressata knows that meat is a business—and especially when that meat is young, sexy, scantily clad female "meat," swirling around strippers poles in G-strings. Every self-respecting mobster should have at least one strip club. Just remember that as a mobster, you're expected to have some class. So be sure to call your strip club a "gentleman's club."

Getting started is easy. There are many young college-age . . . well, *ladies* who have no idea how they're going to foot the tuition bill. They have a need. You have a resource. Just be particular about whom you recruit. If you can, get the depressed philosophy major with a killer body and deep-seated guilt complex. You know the type. Daddy didn't give enough love so she's got to find it pole-dancing in Jersey City.

Another great resource is the divorced—and recently divorced if you can swing it. Look for women no older than say, their mid twenties, and best if they have a couple of noisy toddlers to feed and clothe—and a deadbeat ex-husband, naturally. These women are always behind on the rent or the mortgage—*real* desperate housewives who could use an extra $1,000 a week as long as they don't mind it being shoved into their G-strings.

Take It from Me . . .

Be sure your strippers have names like Tiffany, Britney, Fantasia, Heather, Bambi, Essence, Cheyenne, Destiny, Amber, or Savannah. Those are sexy names. You don't want chicks with names like Hortense, Prunella, Mabel, Agatha, Rosie (as in O'Donnell), Mary Grace, Clementine, or Agnes-Jean. These are your grandmothers' names. And that's a turnoff.

Any strip joint needs a good bouncer for those times when the customers get a little too excited. This is Andy Cigars, a specialist at peeling horny bastards off of pole dancers and tossing them out the door, usually headfirst. (photo courtesy Andrew Lombardozzi)

Next is location. I'm not saying you need to have something on a scale with Tony Soprano's Bada Bing—sometimes smaller is better. More intimate. Your best bet is to find a restaurant that went bust and has a parking lot covered with weeds. The bank will be so hot to unload it for a few thousand down and a five-year lease (which you will have no problems breaking if the operation goes sour) they may even help you get the liquor license. Even an uptight banker likes to look at naked women now and then. Gives them a break from staring at spreadsheets all week.

Liquor License

You're going to need one to keep your clientele half loaded and happy to be blowing their paychecks on lap dances. This means, if the bank can't or won't help, negotiating conditions with local police, citizen groups, and the Department of Alcoholic Beverage Control (ABC).

Getting a liquor license can be expensive. For example, many require an application fee, annual fees, processing fees, late fees, etc. Fees vary between states and may also depend on the type of business you are running. Be prepared to "negotiate," especially with community or church groups who may not be interested in the type of entertainment you will be offering. Take the high road. Be the good guy. Make a nice donation to the local Baptist church or Little League. If this doesn't work, invite them all over to get a look at your club before it opens— and have all your girls handy. Spike their Diet Pepsi with some knockout drugs (chloral hydrate is best), then get some photos of them in compromising positions with your dancers and threaten to send the photos to their wives. It's old but it's reliable.

> **Take It from Me . . .**
>
> Never move any swag (stolen merchandise) in or out of your strip club. This will just give the cops a reason to shut it down. And you don't want that—a strip club is a cash business, which means ripe for skimming.

If all else fails, remember the most powerful weapon in your arsenal: intimidation. In a smaller town, most elected officials, from judges to assemblymen to aldermen or whatever, are often paid little or nothing. So they're going to have regular jobs or own a small business.

Let's say the slob who owns the auto parts store is also a part-time assemblyman. A good, honest, God-fearing family man—exactly the kind of man who'll shit little green apples when you walk into his establishment accompanied by guys like Johnny Sausage and Charlie the Chainsaw. Watch how fast he turns into a tower of Jell-O when you say, "I would consider it a personal favor if you'd help me get a liquor license." Even better, now that you have your hooks into him, you can use his auto parts store to move swag in and out of the stockroom. A win-win situation.

Bouncers

Strip club patrons tend to get very excited and horny watching sexy young women strut their stuff in the buff. Sometimes they get crazy with lust and lunge at the women while they're onstage. It's all too common.

So you're going to need a couple of big guys to wade through the crowd and peel the horny bastards off the performers and see to it they're shown the door, usually headfirst.

Booze

Naturally, you're going to want to stock your joint with the best top-shelf hooch. This is usually the least of your headaches when opening a gentleman's club. Once the liquor salesmen hear you're opening a joint, they'll happily front you a couple hundred cases of Chivas and Stoli on credit so they can get your account.

Health Inspectors, Electrical Inspectors, Building Inspectors, Etc.

Sooner or later, you'll need to deal with these guys. You'd be amazed at the code violations these *stronzos* can find if they look hard enough. In this case, don't argue—bribe. A couple of hundred apiece and a case of Jack Daniel's will usually do the trick.

The Cops

Designate one of your crew to be the "bagman" whose job it is to deliver an envelope full of cash to the chief of police at the first of every month. This will ensure you don't get raided—or worse, shut down.

Garbage Collection

Hire a firm with absolutely no organized crime connections to handle your trash pickups. That way you can move in and steal the business right out from under them. Also, it's good to have a mid-sized trucking company at your disposal. You can buy one or, better yet, steal one.

Closing Thoughts

When it comes to your staff, the best advice you can take is to try not to get too attached. Your crime family is not forever; many of the members you select are simply not going to stand the test of time. They can get offed by rival families. They can get offed by you. Remember: Eventually someone is going to betray you. If it happened to Jesus Christ, it could happen to you.

CHAPTER 5

Mafia Women

or,

Deadlier than the Male?

In Sicily, women are more dangerous than shotguns.
—Calo (Franco Citti), *The Godfather* (1972)

THERE IS SOME TRUTH TO THE FACT THAT MAFIA WOMEN CAN BE tougher, meaner, wield a scary amount of power, and even be deadlier than Mafia males—but their brand of ferocity is never measured in limbs (of others) broken, gunshots fired, or general body counts. These women know where to hit where it hurts: the wallet. And if we're talking about your goomar, there's likely another place she can maim you. But we'll come back to that.

But no matter how ferocious, under no circumstances is a woman permitted to control you. If you have an entire family of captains and associates that know well enough that they are to respect and fear you, so should the women in your life—including your mother and daughter.

Forget how you've dealt with the women in your life in the past. You're a made man now. There's just no way that taking out the garbage is your job anymore. In fact, you no longer have any household chores anymore. Except to keep your family safe from any machine-gun spray intended for you. The house is your wife's domain. If she doesn't like it, don't worry. We'll show you how to make her like it. Remember that creepy suburban town called Stepford? You and your family have just moved in. Only in this case, it ain't called Stepford. It's Gangland, baby!

The main women you'll need to keep a tight leash on are your wife and goomar(s), but we'll give you some insight into the others, too. By the time you finish this section, you'll know how to handle broads in true mafioso style!

At the end of the day, just like any other aspect of your new mobster life, you're not in this to make friends. You're in it for the money and for the sex. People will not always understand this, and that goes especially for your family. So what? You're the boss. You're the breadwinner. As soon as your wife starts reaping the rewards of being a mobster's wife—the jewelry, the clothes, the respect she'll start receiving in the checkout line of the grocery store—she'll start to come around. And remember: The only woman you ever need to keep in your good graces is your goomar.

In this chapter, you will learn:

- The roles of women in a Mafia family—and how to control them.

- How to reprogram your wife into a Mafia wife if you're already married—and how to choose a wife if you're not.

- What you should look for in a goomar—and personality traits that should send you screaming into the night.

Mama Mia!

If you're an Italian male, there's no reason to read this section. If you were born into the life, you know full well how much suffering and sacrifice and sopressata went into "giving you everything I never had."

If you're not, it's time to forget everything you know about your relationship with your mother, who will now be referred to exclusively as your "mama." It doesn't matter if she stayed home to raise you, or if you were raised by a nanny or in daycare—or even temporary foster care. Your mother is now "sainted" and can officially make you feel guilty when you forget to call her several times a week or miss Sunday dinner (which, if your family hasn't had these ever before, will, starting now).

Of course, this is a two-way street—and your mama, no matter how sainted, isn't getting something for nothing. No one is ever getting something for nothing from you ever again. Suggest to Mama these ways that she can help you in your new career, and see how she reacts. You'll finally be able to see whether she truly loves you or not.

A mobster's mama must always wear black.

A mobster's mama must never ask questions about her son's job.

A mobster's mama must just know all the bad things he's up to and go to church daily and pray on her rosary for the fate of her son's soul.

And finally—and this part is 100 percent nonnegotiable—a mobster's mama must be prepared at any time of the day or night to set out a full-course Italian meal when you drop by with your capos, peckish from a night of pillaging and general bad behavior.

If your mother refuses to go along with all of this, it could mean you need to stop talking to her, and then head to a nursing home and convince some lonely, ancient (black-wearing, rosary-praying) Italian woman who's lost some of her marbles that you are, in fact, her son. Or, better yet, your mother could "disown" you for "disgracing" her—which actually would make her a full-fledged Mafia mama after all!

Take It from Me . . .
It is perfectly acceptable to slap, or have slapped, anyone who insults your mama, whether it's done intentionally or not. Even—and especially—if that person happens to be right.

Daddy's Little Girl

Do you remember the episode of *The Sopranos* when Tony's driving Meadow around to look at colleges and she asks him if he's in the Mafia? And that's the last time she ever asks? You want your little girl to be smart, but not too smart. And you don't want her to sass you—especially in public.

Mafia daughters become Mafia wives, and it's your job, as a good father, to make sure your little princess understands when to keep her mouth shut—to only speak when she's been spoken to (and let her mother worry about the rest). Otherwise, she'll be living under your roof until she's sixty.

Here are some tips on how to groom a proper Mafia princess:

Do not let her date non-Italians.

Do not let her date women.

Actually, do not let her date.

Keep her on a strict curfew.

Keep her on a diet.

And, whatever you do, do not let her grow up to become someone's goomar.

The best advice, though, is that if you don't have kids yet, try not to have daughters. The allegiance of your daughter will always be with her husband. And if he happens to be part of a rival family, you're going to be shit-out-of-luck one day. Have sons. They may not be as cute or doting, but it will be much easier to introduce your boy to the back of your hand at the dinner table when he gets out of line.

> ### Take It from Me . . .
> Keep your wife inside the house. If you do bring her out in public, treat her like a queen by holding doors, that kind of thing. But inside the house, you're the king. That means dinner's on the table on time. Or else . . .

That Mrs. Mobster to You

Mafia wives come in many shapes and sizes, but there are very stringent conditions attached to running the house of the capo di capos.

At the top of the list—though not the very top—a mafia wife is expected to be attractive. You need to be married to a woman whom not only can you bed from time to time—at the very least to produce heirs and keep the family line going—but also of whom you'll be proud to show up with at weddings and funerals and other family functions. She should be pretty, but by no means in a flamboyantly sexy way.

That being said, she must be scrupulously faithful. She must be willing to die first before even thinking of sleeping with someone who is not you. Any Mafia wife caught screwing around is subject to face the wrath of the family—and God himself. In biblical times, a woman would be stoned to death in the public square for cheating on her husband. You punish as you see fit. Of course, Mafia men are not similarly encumbered by the vow of fidelity. But we'll get into that a little bit later.

Your wife is expected to be a good housekeeper. No one else should be permitted to come in and clean your house. It's her job, and she should take great pride in gleaming counter-tops and floors the family could eat macaroni and gravy off. And she should be able to whip up a mean macaroni and gravy—even at a moment's notice (see Mama Mia! page 92).

And, in a way, one of the most important attributes: She needs to have mastered the art of knowing what *not* to see. This could be anything from blood to lipstick on your shirt collar or dirt on your "workboots."

The perfect Mafia wife should be attractive, loyal, loving, and understanding—especially when you start collecting mistresses.

Your Kind of Woman

If you're not already married, it's time to get hitched as any self-respecting mafioso is a family man—in every sense of the word. If you are already married, and your wife doesn't seem to be Mafia-wife material, like if she's some kind of career girl or something like that, don't sweat it: there are several strategies to help her to relearn a woman's God-intended place in no time at all, which we'll get into a bit later.

Okay, I can't lie to you. If you're not already married, the road to finding/creating the perfect Mafia wife will be much smoother for you. And speaking of rocky, if your marriage can be described as such already, maybe this is a good time to end it and start over with someone who will really appreciate you and your career goals, and who will do whatever she can to help you achieve them.

Actually, once you become a full-fledged mafioso, a lot of "clutter" in your life is going to disappear. Some, you'll decide to toss to the curb. Some will willingly flee "the monster you've become," and still others, when you get down to business, will simply "disappear." Of course we're not suggesting here that you whack your wife, no matter what you decide to read between the lines.

Mafia Princess

If at all possible, set the daughter of another high-ranking mobster in your sights—a well-trained, already accustomed to the life, bona fide Mafia princess. On the plus side, she's already been conditioned and groomed, psychologically and biologically, to the Mafia lifestyle. She knows what's expected and what to expect from living large and living a life of crime. Like the Midwest has its corn and beef girls, these ladies are all spaghetti and meatballs, cannoli and espresso.

John "Goumba Johnny" Sialiano

Landing a wife like this is like hitting the Mafia Wife Lottery.

But if this is your plan, you're probably better off seeking out one from a different city or state—and the farther away from your state, the better. As long as your wife lives with you, she becomes yours. But she's still Daddy's girl at heart. And nothing can muddy her allegiance to you more than if Daddy's close enough to run home to on a regular basis. Or set you in the sights of his own semiautomatic machine gun.

According to the old ways, your best bet would be to try and marry someone from the family's daughter. And not just any *gavone*, but a high-ranking official. This guaranteed, for the most part, safety and upward mobility—if you didn't fuck up with Daddy's little girl. Because that could mean death. But if you played your cards right—potential elevation within the organization.

No matter what you think you're going to be able to get away with in this situation, always keep in the front of your mind that Daddy's the boss—and she'll use that, too, but only when you push too far. But don't worry. If her daddy did his job, she'll be subservient for the most part. Only an act of gross misconduct will send her running back to Daddy.

Speaking of which . . . your father-in-law will already know about your extramarital and extracurricular activities. As long as you proceed with discretion and respect, you should be okay.

The Woman for Your Average Joe (or Frankie or Paulie)

If you don't get lucky enough to land a Mafia princess, okay. Just proceed with the utmost caution when you wade through the dating pool, and keep your eyes open for qualities that can make an ordinary woman into a Mafia wife. What should you be looking for?

A woman who's smart . . . but not too smart. You want her to understand a thing or two, but you don't want her thinking about taking over.

She should be beautiful . . . but not too beautiful. In other words, if your buddies want to bag her, not so good. And if your buddies have bagged her, she's totally out of the running.

She should be easily malleable. A woman with too-rigid a sense of morality will only trip you up.

She should exhibit a sense of undying loyalty—but only to you. Not to her friends or family members. If a woman is not willing to blow off her friends and family for you, she's not worth a second date.

But, she also needs to be able to spend long periods of time alone. A night, a week, even a month can go by before she may hear from you again, but she must be okay with this. As time goes on, this quality of hers could become more appreciated than her ability to make lasagne.

She should come from a good family, who can keep her company during all your many long and unexplained absences and never-ending business trips to "nowhere."

She needs to accept you being vague and not question it. When you say, "I'm going out," she must show that she knows and fully accepts this means you could be back in ten minutes, later that night, later that week, or just in time for Sunday dinner.

She should be a good networker, but must also be able to prove that she can keep her mouth shut. Yes, you want her to connect with other wives, but you don't want gossip, especially about you, your business, or what goes on—or doesn't go on—in your bedroom.

And finally, she must be a great cook or at least have the willingness and the ability to learn.

Pay close attention to these and you should end up with a woman who has what it takes to put up with you and your chosen path. Otherwise, you'll want to put a hit on yourself the first time you spend the night out with your goomar and your wife greets you at the front door with a frying pan and a look in her eyes that could very well kill you on the spot.

If You're Already Married . . .

Do you know that guy, Cesar Milan, who calls himself "the Dog Whisperer?" To transform your existing wife into a Mafia princess, you'll have to become "the Wife Whisperer."

Your wife is in the embryonic phases of becoming a princess, and for that reason, you need to spoon-feed her bite-size suggestions of the lifestyle and her part in it. She first needs to crawl and walk before she can run with it, so try not to force-feed her if you can help it. Do not expose, inform, or educate at an indigestible pace. The more rewards she begins to receive (see page 102), the more likely it is that she will readily and willingly embrace her new role.

Of course, women these days have their own ideas about a lot of things, and for that reason, your wife may not be that easy to sway. In these extreme cases, you may need to resort to brainwashing, à la *A Clockwork Orange*. Introduce messages slowly and carefully by showing her scenes in mobster movies and TV, but you need to censor what she is and is not to see. Let her see the scene in *The Sopranos* when Adriana gets led to the woods at the end of Silvio Dante's gun for flapping her gums; do not let her watch the scene in *GoodFellas* when Karen Hill harasses Henry Hill's goomar, or straddles him on their bed and holds him at gunpoint for screwing around on her. You get the idea. And never, under any circumstances, let her see an entire film. You don't want her to know too much.

The Mobsters' Wives Hall of Fame—and Shame

GOOD: Apollonia Corleone, Michael Corleone's first wife, was innocent, sweet, with an insatiable appetite to please her new husband. Apollonia would have made the perfect Mafia wife had she not gotten herself blown up.

GOOD: Mama Corleone, Don Corleone's wife, is the ultimate good Mafia wife. Keep the house under control, raise powerful heirs.

GOOD: Janice Soprano was a very good Mafia wife. She was born and raised in the life. She understands.

MEDIUM: Kay Corleone. In the first *Godfather* movie, she was quiet and naive; by the last, she was a total pain in the ass.

MEDIUM: For the most part, Carmela Soprano made for a good Mafia wife. But every now and then, she crossed the line, and Tony was there to get her back on track.

BAD: Connie Corleone, Michael's sister, tried to be good but she was too high strung. Not letting her husband, Carlo, have a goomar caused a lot of unnecessary drama in the family.

VERY BAD: Fredo Corleone's blond bimbo Deanna, got drunk at Michael's son's holy communion and embarrassed the hell out of everyone by getting tanked and falling down on the dance floor. A good Mafia wife *never* gets fall-down drunk.

VERY BAD: Ginger McKenna was the epitome of a bad Mafia wife in *Casino*. Slutty, hustling trophy wife. A great goomar, but a terrible choice for a wife.

"I'm going to tell everybody that walks in this building that in 2R, Rossi, you're nothing but a whore. . . . Is this the superintendent? . . . Yes, sir, I would like you to know that you have a whore living in 2R. . . . He's my husband. Get your own goddamn man."

—Karen Hill (Lorraine Bracco),
GoodFellas (1989)

Take It from Me . . .
Each new lesson should be taught to your wife one at a time. There should be no advancing to the next lesson until she passes the current test. No moving on until she passes the code.

What She Needs from You

You have to give your wife enough information so she can answer all questions posed by neighbors and police about your "legit business holdings"—but nothing further. She needs the ability to cosign your bullshit when it comes to your "legit" businesses. Officially, John Gotti was a plumber, though one wonders if he even knew what a washer was. But if you asked his wife what he did for a living, she'd tell you he fixed pipes.

Information about your other businesses should be provided on a need-to-know basis. She has to be taught the importance of being the woman behind the man, and it's your job to get her to fall into line. Teach her, in whatever way you can, not to ask questions.

Keeping the Peace at Home

To keep your wife happy with the new rules and regime, you're going to have to show her the rewards—cars, a big house, a Jacuzzi tub, and the finest, gaudiest clothes and jewelry money can buy. Everyone will know who her husband is by the way her clothes and jewels drip and ooze off her. She will not be mistaken for a JAP, WASP, or a socialite in any way. When she walks down the street, everyone knows that's Vinny's old lady. Don't even look at her. Not worth it.

The best way to keep her interested in you, and this life you've created for you, is to show her indifference. Nothing says irresistible like indifference (and it will buy you plenty of question-free nights away from home to spend with your goomar).

> TONY MONTANA (Al Pacino): You don't got nothing to do with your life. Why don't you get a job? Work with lepers. Blind kids. Anything's gotta be better than lying around all day waiting for me to fuck you.
> ELVIRA HANCOCK (Michelle Pfeiffer): Don't toot your horn, honey. You're not that good.
> —*Scarface* (1983)

Your Salvation

Some women are born into the life, some marry into it, and some are ready, willing, and unbelievably able to fuck their way into it. You need to find these women—and plenty of them. After all, one of the perks all of the violence and ill-begotten-gains earns you is the right to bed whomever you want, whenever you choose. And the more powerful you are, the younger and hotter the women you'll get—which is incentive enough for many mobsters.

Despite the great personal sacrifice and threat to domestic tranquility that you may incur, you're going to have to force yourself to keep intimate, extramarital company with at least one nice, refined young lady of elegance and taste. (Exotic dancers and nude models are best.) So feel free to seek sexual partners outside the marriage bed. In fact, it's practically mandatory for a mob man to have at least one outside woman. It is expected of you from your associates and underlings—just as much as making money and planning hits. Remember: A man who won't cheat on his wife can hardly be trusted.

The Next Generation

When it comes to continuing the family line, you want to have boys. It's a good practice if you are not already married, or even if you're looking to retire your old wife and seek out an upgrade, to select a wife with a history of boys running through her family. It makes no sense to have this empire if you have no one to leave it to—and you're not going to leave it to some girl. Lastly, try not to procreate with your goomar if you can possibly help it.

Closing Thoughts

Just a word or two on all those heirs your Mafia princess—not your goomar—is going to produce for you: All too often, it's the children of mobsters who destroy the empire. This is because, just as in any other industry, they did not earn it, they are not vested enough in it, they are way too spoiled. Discipline is everything.

Keep in mind that organized crime members who can't control their families are seen as weak. Dysfunctional spouses and kids need to be dealt with, as they will hold you back in your crime career. Take care of this before they are permitted to step outside the house. After all, how can you run the waterfront when you can't control your wife; how can you run the meat market if your kids are a bunch of meatheads?

Discipline starts early. Make sure as soon as your kid is able to discern you from one of his stuffed animals that he knows you are the boss and that you will be his biggest nightmare, and that insolence will never be tolerated. As with everything in mob culture, respect starts in the home.

CHAPTER 6

Cornering a Racket

or,

Mob-enomics 101

For us to live any other way was nuts. Uh, to us, those goody-good people who worked shitty jobs for bum paychecks and took the subway to work every day, and worried about their bills, were dead. I mean they were suckers. They had no balls. If we wanted something we just took it. If anyone complained twice they got hit so bad, believe me, they never complained again.
—Henry Hill (Ray Liotta), *GoodFellas* (1989)

HAVE YOU EVER DREAMED OF JUST SITTING BACK WHILE PILES OF MONEY came at you for basically doing nothing—except, of course, orchestrating a little careful intimidation and a lot of someone else's muscle?

Making money is the number one reason anyone decides to become a mobster and, if you play your cards right (or set up your gambling operations correctly), that's just what you'll get.

What you need to do is to corner some rackets, as many as you can, because no self-respecting mafioso would ever work for a living. Not only would it be a humiliation, your street cred would be shot to hell. Can you imagine Tony Soprano pushing paperwork in some office somewhere—or driving a bus? Fuggedabouddit! You can set up a front to make it look like you've got something legitimate going on, but you must never actually do manual labor or pointless paperwork.

What you need to do is find someone else who is working for a living—any kind of a living, legitimate or otherwise, as long as it generates revenue—and "persuade" that person to pay you to let them go on working and living. We'll get into the finer details as we move through this chapter, but that's pretty much all there is to it.

Just watch your step that you don't actually invade any true Mafia territory. Unless you savor the prospect of being made into dog food, put in cans, and distributed to a national chain of pet stores. But don't let that discourage you. There's plenty of opportunity for everyone. You just need to be creative, open minded, and resourceful about the business you tap.

In this chapter, you will learn:

- How to use mob-enomics to amass your own felonious fortune

- Failsafe formulas for making the usual well-established, ever-dependable revenue-generators work

- Plus, innovative, fresh, exciting, and virtually untapped markets to target for your own criminal enterprise

---

Wiseguys in the Mainstream

Arnold Rothstein is a character in *The Great Gatsby*, but he's called Meyer Wolfsheim, "the man who fixed the 1919 World Series."

Minding Your Business

Racketeering works a lot like the corporate world. Except, in corporate America, everything is done "legally." Or at least stretched to the very limits of the written law. In Gangland, there are only three laws you need to pay attention to: Get in there, get yours, get out without getting yourself killed.

But in reality, the only difference between you and the average CEO is that you're labeled "made," while he churns out products with the "made in America" logo. But don't be fooled. These guys are just as bad as you—in some cases, they are worse. And you are actually the better person, as you at least are upfront about what you're doing.

The big difference is in how you make your money. CEOs are usually limited to selling the product, and it's usually something their company specializes in. You don't need to specialize. Generalize! Corner as many markets as you can! It's easy, really. Take a look around you right now as you read this book. What do you see? Maybe a TV and stereo, a bottle of wine, cigarettes, candles, the couch you're sitting on, the litter box.

Everything that can be bought and sold is an opportunity for you to make money, and that includes human beings. As an added bonus, you'll be amazed by how much free stuff will start coming your way. You'll never have to *buy* your wife another anniversary present ever again!

Take It from Me . . .

As a mobster, know that opportunity will knock daily, so you'll have to pick and choose the businesses you want to get involved in. Before jumping into a racket, take the time to consider which product and fields interest you most, and which will most appeal to your higher ups, if you have any.

Simple Mob-enomics

The easiest way for a mobster to make money, which is probably why it's the most common, is through simple "interference"—which is also sometimes referred to as "extortion." Your goal is to get in the middle of any business deal you can and institute a Mafia tariff. Ideally, you want to squeeze out 10 percent from the buyer, 10 percent from the seller, and an additional 10 percent from anyone else who may be involved in the deal.

Let's go through an example of mob-enomics in action. Let's say Joe sells candles for a living. He has no Italian friends. He sells his candles for a dollar a piece to Tom, who sells them for two dollars each, retail. Tom also has no Italian friends.

For Joe to get on-time, guaranteed shipping, with no merchandise stolen or broken—or limbs broken for that matter—he'll gladly offer up a percentage of his earnings for protection from these potential catastrophes.

And for Tom to ensure that his candles arrive on time, his shelves are properly stocked, and his garbage is picked up on time—with the bones of his legs and those in the legs of his employees remaining intact—he will also gladly pay into the insurance policy you're offering. There you have it: You're in business and you haven't had to buy or sell or outlay anything.

Evaluating Business Interests

When deciding which markets you should be tapping into, approach the situation just as a legitimate businessman would, looking into those factors essential to making any business thrive:

- Supply and demand—and how you'll be creating both
- Sources of supply—and how to make sure you corrupt the ones you don't want and build the ones you do
- Pricing decisions—in terms of how big a percentage you feel you are entitled to

- Markups and markdowns—which, translated into mob terms, is calculated in how much slack you're going to afford some *gavone* who owes you money before enforcement tactics are employed

"Fuck you, pay me."
—**Henry Hill (Ray Liotta)**, *GoodFellas* (1989)

Getting Started

What you need to do is to create a need. That way, you can provide a service that hadn't been needed before, like becoming the middleman between Tom and Joe, and capitalize on it. Here's how to do it.

Approach Joe, wearing your best suit and flanked by two of your spookiest-looking goons. Tell him you've been watching his business and that you think he'd be much better off if he had a partner. He'll tell you he doesn't need a partner. You'll change his mind. How?

In the weeks that follow, all of Joe's trucks will be hijacked. His stock will be looted and his merchandise will be smashed to smithereens. Soon, his business will begin to spiral. There will be no way for him to make up his losses. His wife will threaten to leave him. Perhaps some of his hair will fall out from the stress. Congratulations. You have now completed Step 1. You have made it rain.

Way back in his memory banks, as he's drinking too much and possibly planning his own suicide, Joe will remember a conversation he had with you—and about how you made him an offer he should never have refused. He'll pray that your price hasn't skyrockted too much. He will greet you with open arms. And you will hug him back with a 10 percent increase on your original offer.

Next, Tom will be faced with similar problems. He'll know about Joe's hard times and see his miraculous recovery. And to save his marriage and his liver and his life, he'll ask Joe how he pulled through—and Joe will be ready with a sterling recommendation. And now Tom will also have Italian friends.

Voilà! You're now a full partner in the candle wholesale and retail business. What do you get to enjoy?

- A guaranteed income
- Free holiday gifts for family, friends, and associates—not to mention your goomar
- Gainful employment for friends, associates, and relatives, who you can now afford to pay handsomely for watching over your business interests

---

Take It from Me . . .

If you're getting started working for someone else, feed him what he eats. For example, does your boss have a penchant for cars?

To improve your status in the family and get in good with the boss, corner a car dealership and get him cars. If you ever get into trouble with the boss, a good collection of businesses that cater to his interests and tastes are like Band-Aids to heal these wounds.

Networking, Mafia Style!

As you build your empire, remember that businesses feed off each other, like the case with Tom and Joe. For that reason, you want to network, and heavily. The candle seller does business with the candle buyer, but each of these legit losers does business with so many others. Who supplies their paper? Who's cleaning the warehouse and office spaces? Who's picking up the trash? All of these businesses can be (silently) controlled by you.

A good way to make connections with all these business is to get in with the staff. Disgruntled employees are your ticket in. While you offer them a shoulder to cry on, they'll show you the cracks in the foundation of the business they work in. Become almost like the parish priest. Listen to all the gripes of employees. No matter how well they're treated, someone will always have something to complain about. Turn their lemons into your lemonade.

Once you get the wheels of mob-enomics rolling, you won't be able to keep up with the number of opportunities presented to you.

Discreet Business Communication

Always assume that the FBI or some other government *gavones* have tapped your phones, both at home and in your social club. Hence, it's necessary to discuss business using as few incriminating words as possible, or devising a secret code that would have the bright boys at the NSA scratching their asses.

Wrong: "Did you talk to Jimmy Bones about those cases of hijacked booze we were expecting Monday morning at the club?"

Right: "Did you talk to the guy about the thing?"

Wrong: "Did you whack 'Tony Meatballs' like I said and chop up his body and dump it in Willie Cheech's landfill?"

Right: "Did you take care of that thing for me downtown?"

Speak smart, and you stay in business. Speak stupid, and watch your empire fall. It's that easy.

Opportunity Abounds!

Now that you have a basic understanding of the blueprint for mob-enomics, the world is your oyster. Speaking of oysters, the fish market has been very good to mobsters throughout the years. In fact, any perishable goods business is a good tap—be it pizza, fish, or groceries. Any business with deadlines and/or expiration dates is an excellent target. You need to find places where you can play on desperation, and these types of time-sensitive businesses are perfect. For example, without refrigeration, the grocer's going to get stuck with a lot of rotting food. Without a cheese delivery, how can the pizza man make his pies?

Remember: First create the problem, then offer the solution. And hey, you may get really lucky sometimes. Instead of your having to get involved in their daily operations, there may be some small businessmen who will actually pay you just to stay away from them!

Traditionally, the most common industries for mobsters have been:

- waste management
- construction
- restaurants and nightclubs
- petroleum
- garment industry
- fish markets
- financing, a.k.a. lending
- gambling
- prostitution
- import/export
- Hollywood

Actually, it's hard to think of an industry the mob hasn't infiltrated. But to ensure success, for your operation, you're going to have to think outside the box and target the rich surplus of untapped markets in your own neighborhood:

- Charities and nonprofits—they're flourishing in light of all the turmoil in the world

- Church functions—it's not like they really *need* another Mary statue

- Health care—go ahead and shake down your physician and his buddies. Actually, the HMOs already have that one cornered

- Paparazzi protection—a term with two meanings, which means a two-way street for you when you can get paid to protect the celebrities and the shutterbugs

- Birthday parties, sweet sixteens, bar and bat mitzvahs— have you seen the cash that goes into those envelopes these days?!

- Your kids' next school bake sale or even the fourth grade play . . . oh, the possibilities!

The point is you need to do your research and watch the trends as they arise. Here's an example. Dogs and dog accessories are hot this year—especially for those small, annoying dogs. How can you get a piece of that action? Do you have a big chain pet store in your neighborhood (not recommended) or a privately owned boutique pet store (highly recommended)? And what about the whole wellness industry? Vitamin shops, juice bars, yoga studios—these kinds of establishments are nearly always privately owned by very earthy, spiritual types who don't know much about how businesses are run and can really use your help—and also get the whole "mortality" thing. What dif-

---

Take It from Me . . .
Always target independently owned businesses—the less existing partners to deal with, the better. Stay far away from federal businesses. In addition to courting disaster, there really isn't enough money in them to tempt that kind of danger.

ference does it make where the money comes from, as long as it comes!

Just keep your eye on the prize and seize the day whenever you can. Whatever you choose, the standard formula applies: Make the problems, then offer the solutions. It's all very simple. You open up a flat-fixing store off the highway, and also get involved in the business of the guy who sells nails. Very basic. Just smart business.

Talk the Talk, Part 3

Here's more mob lingo to add to your words arsenal and keep the only interference in your business ventures the type that you create.

Clip: The term for making money off someone else. Both Tom and Joe got clipped by you in the candle scenario. (Nice work!)

Case: Another word for scouting out business interests. Before you decide to dive in to a particular venture, you'll want to "case" it to make sure it can make you a viable living—and not too closely connected to an organization that can stop you in your tracks (like the IRS).

Envelope: This is what you call the cash payment your underlings will be collecting for you from your various business interests. "Did you get the envelope?" "The envelope is not as fat this week." You get the idea.

Fence: A person you work with who specializes in handling your stolen merchandise—that is, merchandise you or your organization has stolen.

Juice: Think of it this way—the later the payback, the juicier the reward. You never loan money without charging interest—not even to your elderly aunt—and the juice is any interest owed to you on that loan (see page 118 for more about loan-sharking).

Large: Wiseguyspeak for "one thousand" in money. If someone owes you thirty large, that's $30,000. (And if someone owes you that kind of cash, it's time to bring in your Enforcer to collect it).

Make a marriage: Just as two people get locked in a partnership when they get married, so do two parties doing business. If you want to get involved in someone else's business, refer to it as "making a marriage." It's much easier on the ears than "extortion."

Some Popular Rackets

The next sections of this book will look at some of the opportunities you may decide to capitalize on. We've already looked at extortion as a way to make quick cash. Here are a couple more.

Gambling

As a mobster, you can and should take bets on anything. Gambling is a very easy way to make money, especially when you can turn the odds in your favor.

When betting on the ponies, it's possible that with your help, the sure-bet horse will mysteriously lag behind the pack, while the underdog shoots ahead. As a mobster, look into rigging horse races, dog races, college sports, high school sports, even Gymboree competitions if they have them. Any person or any person controlling an animal has a price. Always remember this.

Your job becomes that much easier when it's a craps table or roulette wheel or slot machine that needs rigging, as these operate without conscience or any semblance of morality.

Keep in the front of your mind that people love to gamble

and you should exploit this. But not everyone can get to Vegas or Atlantic City to satisfy these cravings, and this is another thing you can and must exploit. Establish an illegal casino over a Chinese restaurant, a Laundromat, or even in the back of your own social club. The location doesn't have to be glamorous—it just can't be too obvious.

Just be sure that when you do open your casino that you provide 24/7 access to gambling. People, and especially people with a gambling problem, will sometimes need to sneak out in the middle of the night, without their wives or husbands or parents or kids knowing what they're up to. Remember supply and demand: If someone has a demand to gamble at 3:30 A.M., someone needs to be the one to supply him a way to blow his hard-earned cash. Why not you?

Loan-Sharking

Loan-sharking works like extortion, except you don't have to bother yourself with the many details involved when you bring merchandise and overhead into the picture. With loan-sharking, it's all about pure cash. How does it work?

Here's an example. John needs $500 to buy Christmas presents for his family. John has a drinking problem and is not good with saving money because he prefers to drink his paycheck away than let it collect dust in the bank. But it's now December 15, and John has saved no money for presents. And he's already been threatened to be thrown out of the house should he fuck up again. John needs help. Lucky for John, he likes having Italian friends.

John comes to you for help and, of course, you're more than happy to help him. You're his friend, after all. He's seen you bail others out of cash binds, so why not him. You're like the friendly neighborhood cash machine. And unlike other lenders, you're a trusting sort. You require no credit reports or background checks. You're more than willing to make a "gentleman's agreement." There's no long interview process—nothing to waste the precious time John just doesn't have at this point.

You lend him the $500 he needs and, because you are a businessman, which he will understand, you'll do this by charging him on a system of points. If you charge him five points on $500, that means he'll to pay you $25 per week until he can pay back the original $500 in one lump sum (there are no installment payments here).

The good news for him is that he doesn't actually have a due date to come up with $500 all at once. Now he can keep drinking. This is exceptional news for you as he will never, ever in his life have $500 all at once because he will never stop drinking. So for a onetime payout of $500, he will be paying you an additional $25 a week for the rest of his life.

John's a great bet (see Gambling, page 117) because he's got a city job and steady employment. He gets paid every two weeks. And he drinks every day. He'll eventually end up paying you $25 a week for years—and maybe even borrow another $500 next Christmas.

And surely you know many people like this, and they know many people as well. So while $25 a week for doing nothing may not seem like a lot, $500 or $1,000 per week, still doing nothing, starts looking pretty good. And remember: This is just the interest!

How can you find a guy like John? Chances are you worked with guys like this in your old life when you were a workaday schmuck. Get back in touch with some old friends who may be down on their luck. Buy 'em a few drinks, and see if they have any friends. Once you've put together a couple dozen of these losers, you'll have several thousand dollars in unreportable cash income coming to you weekly. We call this: "Putting money out on the street."

Don't think people are this stupid? Then how do you explain the success of credit card companies?

As your business grows, you'll probably need to hire a "bag man" to collect your interest for you. That's okay. As your enterprise grows, you'll be gaining cash through so many opportunities, you won't know what to do with your money. And maybe that schmuck your sister married can finally find a use for himself in your life.

> DOMINIC MANETTA (Joseph Rigano): Times are
> changing. You've got to change with the times.
> BOSS PAUL VITTI (Robert DeNiro): What, am I
> supposed to get a fuckin' Web site?
> —*Analyze This* (1999)

Mob Lawyers: What to Look For

Okay, so a guy in your crew—let's call him Bobby Bananas—is busted for running a numbers operation out of a pizzeria. Bobby Bananas has got a rap sheet longer than Route 66 and he's looking at a ten-to-fifteen stretch in the can. Under those circumstances, he's an excellent candidate to flip and rat you out in exchange for a lighter sentence or even the Witness Protection Program.

Your options are few. You can buy off a jail guard (affectionately referred to by inmates as "screws") to slip some strychnine into Bobby Bananas' Kool-Aid before he can go to trial—but then you run the risk of the guard being caught and naming you as the one who bribed him. In which case you'll be sharing that cell with Bobby Bananas.

No, your safest bet is to hire a good lawyer to get Bobby Bananas off the hook. If only to prove to the rest of your crew that you'll support them if they get pinched, which, let's face it, is a common occurrence in mobdom.

Here's what to look for in a lawyer:

- He formerly served in the public defender's office before going into private practice and knows all the players.
- Whenever possible, he should be Jewish and belong to the same synagogue and country club as the judges and the district attorney.
- He should be from a blue-collar, working-class family on the wrong side of the tracks who worked his way through law school doing odd jobs for the mob and thus will have sympathy for his client.
- He should know which judges are predisposed to showing wiseguys leniency and which are hardasses who love putting away mobsters for thirty-year stretches.
- He should know which judges can be bought off and which cannot.
- He should have extensive experience in either bribing or intimidating juries.
- He should have a mole in the DA's office who has access to important paperwork.
- It's crucial for your lawyer to have a sleazy private detective (preferably a retired cop) on his payroll.
- If the prosecuting attorney or the DA has any weaknesses that can be exploited (such as hanging out in transvestite bars in full drag or a habit of trying to lure twelve-year-old girls on Internet chat rooms), a good mob lawyer will know about them—this is where a sleazy private eye is worth every penny— and be prepared to expose these habits at the trial.
- A good lawyer will know when the time is right for his wiseguy client to show up at his trial in a mobile hospital bed with an attachable oxygen tank so the lawyer can say to the judge, "Your Honor, my client is not a well man . . ."

This is Sammy Zuckerman, the best mob lawyer in the business. He's smart, he's shrewd, and he plays golf with the district attorney and several judges. He costs plenty, but he'll keep you out of the joint. (photo courtesy Jeffrey Gurian)

Closing Thoughts

There are lots of rackets you may consider—there could be a whole book written on those alone. This chapter, however, is just meant to get you started. If you decide you want to get into prostitution or strip clubs or labor racketeering or tanning parlors or narcotics or even industries already cornered by other mobsters, just remember the same rules always apply: Get in there, get yours, and get out before you get caught. Also, create the need, and be the only one in town who can satisfy it—or piggyback on another operation already set up to do just that. Try these formulas with any venture and you'll never go wrong, no matter what the circumstances. And good luck!

CHAPTER 7

Perfecting the Art of Violence

or,

Kill or Be Killed

Richie loved to use .22s because the bullets are small and they don't come out the other end like a .45, see, a .45 will blow a barn door out the back of your head and there's a lot of dry cleaning involved, but a .22 will just rattle around like Pac-Man until you're dead.

—Vinnie Antonelli (Steve Martin), *My Blue Heaven* (1990)

HERE'S A DIRTY LITTLE SECRET: IT'S NOT REALLY THE FAST MONEY, FASTER women, and lurid lifestyle that are the main draw of the Mafia lifestyle—not once you get yourself fully ensconced in it. Yeah, the other stuff is great, but the ultimate seductive appeal lies in the ability to have a couple of thugs beat hell out of your neighbor when his dog craps on your lawn. Talk about "setting boundaries"!

By you, for you, against you. A mobster lives by the sword or the gun or the knife or the ice pick or the . . . Well, you get the picture. A true made man lives by violence, and dies by the same.

It doesn't matter who you are or how strong your track record is. You can be killed, maimed, or otherwise disfigured at any given moment. It can happen to you—just as it has happened to just about all the greats. And you can be called upon to perform a necessary act of violence at any time. Just remember: Strongarm tactics and the ability to use them define your gangland empowerment and entitlement. In the Mafia, acts of violence are strong résumé builders.

As you move through your career in organized crime, note that the violence you will encounter can be extremely unpredictable. Did Bobby really think he'd get offed in a hobby shop in *The Sopranos'* finale? Would Sonny Corleone have driven through that tollbooth in *The Godfather* if he knew he was gonna eat sixteen pounds of bullets? Of course not. What about all those guys that got hit and whose bodies were found during the "Layla" montage of *GoodFellas*. Do you think any of them woke up that morning thinking: "Later today I'm going to get my brains blown out and hang from a meat hook in a freezer truck!" And come on . . . Tommy DeVito could have avoided having half his head blown off, at least for a while, had it occurred to him that there was no way he was really going to get made . . .

In this chapter, you will learn:

- When violence is necessary and sometimes even fun
- Important tools of the trade no mobster should be without
- How best to dispose of a body—and what are some of the worst ways

Wiseguys in the Mainstream

Hyman Roth's character in *The Godfather, Part II* was based on Meyer Lansky. After seeing the film, legend had it that Lansky called the actor (Lee Strasberg) who played Roth to compliment him on his performance, adding: "You could've made me more sympathetic."

When Is Violence Necessary?

In a word: Always. When you're a mobster, you must think of violence like the air you breathe or the water that sustains you or like the nourishment you get from your mama's meat sauce. Committing acts of violence is as natural to a mobster as crying is to a baby; if you have no stomach for it, maybe it's time to head back to school for that MBA, because you're just never gonna make it as a mobster without bloodlust.

In Gangland, violence is your way in and your way out. No matter how many rackets you're running or what car you're driving or how many goomars you may be juggling, you are not officially a mobster until you commit an act of violence. You don't need to kill someone to get in, but it will catapult you to the top pretty quickly after your initiation if you do. Breaking someone's digits or legs, beating someone with a baseball bat, even blowing up a car—or getting some goon to do any of these for you—is the price of admission. And, if you're lucky, you'll go out in a blaze of glory, a decorated hero in a gang war—a mob lore legend.

Violence is the manure of organized crime. It serves the same purpose as the type you sprinkle on your tomatoes: it helps your operation thrive. If you only threaten violence and never enact it, you will never earn the fear and respect you so richly

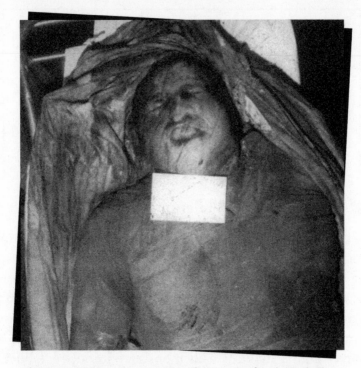

Violence and the mob go together like spaghetti and meatballs or sausage and peppers. This poor bastard is Ricky "Big Balls" Moretti—he got his nickname because he liked to have sex with a lot of different women—until the day he hopped into the sack with his capo's wife and said good-bye to his balls. (photo courtesy U.S. Attorney's Office, Eastern District of New York)

deserve. Without manure, your tomatoes may grow, but they'll be puny and unimpressive as compared to the tomatoes you'll grow with manure.

What Is Violence Used For?

Just like in the animal kingdom, violence in the world of the mob is used to establish territory. Violence settles boundary disputes and make those around you understand where your lines are drawn—and, of course, keeps them in line.

For a mobster, territory is mostly about money and possessions, but it's also about business. No mobster who respects the lifestyle would step in on another's business interests. There may be a suggestion, sure, but you'd be hard pressed to find members of a rival family drinking and flirting with the exotic dancers at your strip club. And that's because of violence. If others disrespect and disregard your territory, you will be well within your rights to take action.

What it all comes down to is money. Violence spurs income and protects the cash you already have. It is used both for financial gain and to maintain financial security, regardless of whether the violence takes the form of a hit, a rubout, a humiliating public slapping.

Can I Use Violence Daily . . . and Still Be a Good Christian?

Absolutely. In the Mafia culture, there's a true double standard when it comes to your business affairs and your sense of spirituality. You may decide to whack someone or be asked to whack someone on a Saturday night; by no means does that mean you'll be excused from attending mass Sunday morning.

But maybe it's not such a double standard after all. If killing was really that bad, would God really have named it Commandment Number Six—out of ten? That's not even the top half. (Neither is stealing, by the way, which clocks in at number eight.) Way more mandatory than not killing is loving and respecting God, the ultimate boss of bosses, above all—and loving and respecting him so much that the first three Commandments are exclusively about loving, respecting, and fearing him.

By the way, your kids not sassing you comes in at four; what you do with your goomar—all the way up at seven.

God is the ultimate mobster.

When you consider all the smiting and the Great Flood and all the violence in the Bible, it's obvious that God gets it—the indisputable necessity of violence to get the job done.

Take It from Me . . .

Do not fear getting shot, as long as the wound isn't fatal. Just as rappers arrange to get shot in the leg or the ass because it's good for record sales, so it is with mobsters. Getting shot is good for business: Not only does it give you credibility, it buys your family favors.

Now the first time you kill somebody, that's the hardest. . . . The second one . . . the second one ain't no fuckin' Mardis Gras either, but it's better than the first one 'cause you still feel the same thing, y'know . . . except it's more diluted. . . . I threw up on the first one, you believe that? Then the third one . . . the third one is easy, you level right off. . . . Now . . . shit . . . now I do it just to watch their fuckin' expression change.

—Virgil (James Gandolfini), *True Romance* (1993)

Killer Style

Mobsters aren't random butchers, and you should always remember this. Those mobsters who kill and maim and torture for the hell of it aren't true mobsters, and are usually offed pretty quickly—and usually by members of their own family.

Think of mobsters not as monsters but as warrior poets. A mobster does not just torture, he tortures with meaning. There is no maiming without an underlying message. There is no killing just for the hell of it.

Mobsters are masters of wit in their violence, and you need to concentrate on this aspect of it when you plan your attacks.

Think of violence as a creative outlet—as well as a necessary and pleasurable perk of your profession. The way you kill, maim, and wound becomes your signature. It could even earn you a cool nickname. For instance, do you like to bash things to a bloody pulp? Then others might start calling you "Frankie the Hammer." As we covered before, nothing sticks like a nickname, so be sure to take great pains in planning your targets, reasons, and methods.

Retiring an Old Favorite: The Telephone

Up until the mid 1980s or so, the telephone made for a great weapon. It was bulky and heavy with all the wiring and mechanisms for ringing making the standard model at least five pounds—if not more. Hurled at someone with just the right amount of rage, it could do a lot of damage. And then there was the cord. The wonderful, fusilli-like cord that could strangle anyone within minutes. Now? Well, that's another story.

Technology, with its fancy microchips and cordless magic has rendered this classic obsolete in the world of mob violence. Ever try and smash someone with a cordless phone? The receiver gives out long before the bones—and who ever heard of someone being killed by plastic splinters? Then there's the cellular phone. What the hell are you supposed to do with that? Strap it to someone's head and wait years for the brain cancer to come? Maybe choke someone to death on their Bluetooth earpiece. Christ, you can't even whack someone in a phone booth anymore. Not only can you not find one anywhere—who would be using it if you did?

Don't worry—there are still plenty of murderous alternatives lying around your house. Check the list on page 133 and get those deadly creative juices flowing.

Violence = Mobster Therapy

On *The Sopranos*, each week mob boss Tony would dutifully kept his appointment with Dr. Melfi, and his mental state never seemed to improve. What would have helped him more is if he had killed more people with his bare hands. Just his offing of his pesky nephew, Christopher, freed him of so much bullshit emotional baggage he'd been carrying around all of those years. In the last episodes, and especially after Melfi showed him the door, he really came into his own.

Of course the average person may find this hard to believe, and that's why a made man is no average person, but a successful hit is a true "feel-good moment" for a mobster. When it's a gang effort, it could even result in a group hug.

For the mobster, violence is a catharsis. It's a necessary release of pent-up rage and emotion that only bogs your business brain down and screws up the works.

Violence also provides a necessary sense of self-affirmation. It gives a sense of purpose, a feeling of control. Just the threat that you will do something to someone makes them do whatever they can to make you happy. And that feels good. It feels right. It's the height of sensory satisfaction. When you kill (or maim, or wound) you are one with the Mafia universe.

Incidentally, the ability to kill people close to you, including workers and colleagues, is essential. If you have the nerve to hand out a pink slip, you need to feel the same ease for pulling a trigger. You can't fire subordinates in the Mafia; you have to take them out. So if you're the kind of guy who brings a person flowers before you have to fire him, perhaps this job ain't for you.

Talk the Talk, Part 4

Never is there a better time to speak in mobster code than when it comes to violence. Of course, the feds are on to most of these terms, so when ordering a hit or even a "gentle reminder" to a business associate behind on his payments, you may want to make up some of your own words. Just make sure your people know what the hell you're talking about if you do.

Biscuit: A code word for what should be more like an appendage than an object you consider separate from you: your gun.

Clean: When you're not carrying a gun—which should only be when you're getting clean. Like in the shower. Even then, you should keep it close by.

Hit: When used in a sentence: "Put a hit on Charlie" or "Old Paulie Two-Times got hit." It's either used to order a killing, or to refer to a killing that's already taken place.

Enforcer: Probably the guy you call "Crazy," this is the family member who carries out your orders to maim, maul, whack, dismember, or what have you.

Piece: Another, more common term for *gun*. Even your grandmother knows this one.

Turban: What it's called when you crack someone's head open. If you want one of your underlings to bust open someone's brain bucket, you tell them: "Give him a turban."

Serious headache: The migraine no medicine will ever cure, this is a nice way of saying someone got a bullet in the head.

Serious trouble: If you ever find out you're in "serious trouble," you'd better go into hiding and quick. It means someone has a contract out on you, and you're about to get whacked.

Whack: The most commonly used term by a mobster for killing someone or ordering someone to be killed.

Tools of the Trade

Every mobster should have a gun or knife in his arsenal of weapons, but these should not be the be-all-end-all. There are so many ways to inflict pain on another human being, so many ways to slaughter a pig.

A gun is quick and efficient, but if your gripe is personal— say, you need to whack someone who took out your favorite uncle or brother—you just won't derive the same satisfaction from shooting someone as you would from some other long, painful, and highly sadistic method.

Following are some nonstandard tools you should consider keeping in your weapons arsenal. The best part about most of these is that if you get pulled over and your car gets searched, they're much easier to explain than, say, a semiautomatic machine gun.

- *An ice pick.* Nothing says "fun-gool" like an ice pick in the throat.

- *A baseball bat.* And make it a wooden (pros don't use aluminum).

- *A tire iron.* It's in your car already. You use it to twist lug nuts, so it's not such a stretch to "break someone's nut" with it.

Take It from Me . . .
Many luxury cars now come equipped with run-flat tires and 24/7 roadside assistance, so depending on what type of car you drive—and it should be a luxury car—a tire iron may not be readily available to you. However, trunks are bigger and more convenient than ever before.

- *Golf clubs.* Golf "clubs" are aptly named and should be used as such. And the longer the club, the more damage it can do. Break off the end and stab your enemy with the shaft. With a shorter club, you can swing away to your heart's content and treat your enemy to a delightfully prolonged and torturous death.

- *Garden tools, such as shovels, picks, and hoes.* The large versions of these are great for body disposal, but the smaller versions, like in those cutesy sets you'd buy for your wife for her birthday, are both portable and effective. Just imagine a wee little garden rake sticking out of the cold, dead forehead of someone who's wronged you.

- *An ax.* A great thrill, all that chopping. But with someone who's still alive, this could get very messy. You may just want to save this tool for body disposal (see page 136).

- *Yards and yards of rope.* Rope is great for restraining, but also for strangulation.

- *Gags and blindfolds.* A skilled and crafty mobster knows that gags and blindfolds come in many shapes and forms. A tie or belt are great standard blindfolds; duct tape is a bit more out of the box. And there's no gag known to man that's more effective than a rolled-up dirty sock in the mouth.

- *Duct tape.* Gag, blindfold, method of restraint, suffocation device, tourniquet, and it can hold your side-view mirror on (temporarily) should someone clip it (or should you knock off your own mirror by running someone down in the road). Duct tape truly does do it all.

- *Words.* You can't necessarily kill with them, but think of all the torture and intimidation a few carefully chosen words can provide.

It helps to have at least one guy in your crew with the nickname "Crazy," like Crazy Joe Gallo. Here's Crazy Dominick. He walks around in his bathrobe and mutters to himself and pisses on mailboxes so the feds will think he's insane. He's also a master with a cattle prod and a blowtorch. (photo courtesy U.S. Attorney's Office, Eastern District of New York)

It's a fact that most any common household item can become a lethal weapon. Violence is really an improvisational science, and the more creative you are, the more effective—and evasive, in terms of getting caught—you will be.

> ### Take It from Me . . .
> Here's where that guy in your gang called "Crazy" will really come in handy. You'll wish you had a dozen like him.

Walk around your home and take a good look around. Seek out normal, innocent objects, and dream up all kinds of evil purposes for them. Most violence that occurs in a house or apartment will occur on the spur of the moment, so it will help you to be prepared with at least a preliminary idea of things you can readily grab—a lamp, a trophy, the business end (that is, the antlers) of a taxidermed deer, et cetera.

With a ballpoint pen, you can write your mama a birthday card; with a ballpoint pen, you can pluck out the eyes of someone who witnessed you doing something no one was ever meant to see. Speaker wire allows sound to flow throughout your home; speaker wire prevents blood flow to your enemy's brain when tightly pulled around his neck. You can use a cast-iron skillet to fry up sausage, peppers, and onions; you can use a cast-iron skillet to give someone a turban (see page 131). A CD broken in half is like a switchblade . . . You get the idea. Just let your imagination run wild!

And remember, at the end of the day, the biggest weapon of all can be your killer smile.

> *There's a lot of holes in the desert, and a lot of problems are buried in those holes. But you gotta do it right. I mean, you gotta have the hole already dug before you show up with a package in the trunk. Otherwise, you're talking about a half-hour to forty-five minutes worth of digging. And who knows who's gonna come along in that time? Pretty soon, you gotta dig a few more holes. You could be there all fuckin' night.*
> —Nicky Santoro (Joe Pesci), *Casino* (1995)

Body Disposal

In the good old days, body disposal was a mindless act. All you needed to do was tie up your kill, then weigh it down with cement bricks and rope, borrow a friend's boat, and toss it overboard. But over the past twenty years or so, body disposal has become very difficult, for several reasons.

In addition to significant advances in technology that make nailing down evidence more easy for law enforcement, there's that damned surge in real estate development, which has all but obliterated desired wetlands. And not to mention the craze over recycling and waste management, which makes it nearly impossible to drop a body off at the dump, where it will never be seen again.

But the worst of all have been the popularity of crime and forensic TV shows. Now everyone and his mother will know how to find you.

Don't worry. There are ways to actually make these obstacles work for you—or at least what I'll refer to as the *CSI* factor. Just beat them at their own game.

Pay attention to what you see on TV. Watch *CSI*—every single episode ever made. Not only will it provide you with the means and circumstances to kill and hide a body and not get caught—as you can see how others screwed up and got themselves busted—it will show you the latest advances in forensics, thereby teaching you how to properly cover your tracks. At least two hundred hours is the recommended amount of viewing before perpetrating a crime in which a body must be hidden.

Method and Madness

How you go about disposing of a body has everything to do with the person you are—it's all about your personality, your threshold for gore, and, quite frankly, your skill set.

If you like it neat, don't dismember—bury in the ground or the sea. If you're a sucker for guts, by all means, chop away. And if you're especially sadistic, nothing quite satisfies like limbs bubbling away in a tub of sulfuric acid. And then there are your skills. If you have a bad back and can't wield an ax, don't chop. On the other hand, if you're a master with a buzz saw, run with it. The best favor you can do for yourself is to stick with what you know. You don't go to the dentist when your back hurts, right?

Most important, learn from the mistakes of others—both real and what you see on TV. Pay scrupulous attention to how others have gotten themselves caught. Don't repeat their mistakes. It's just that easy.

> ### *Take It from Me . . .*
> These days, even duct tape has a serial number and can be traced back to your purchase. Be careful!

No Stone Left Unturned

Once you've gotten rid of your little problem, take great care to cover your tracks. Make plenty of room for reasonable doubt. Even if this means planting absurd evidence. Remember: There is no statute of limitations on murder, and the life you save could be your own.

Top Tools for Body Disposal

- *Cinderblocks.* An oldie but goodie, cinderblocks will weigh down any enemy—no matter how much pasta he's eaten in his lifetime.
- *Plastic bags.* Don't go for generics. You don't want a wimpy bag that leaks blood and bile and brain matter everywhere. Invest in the highest-quality trash bag money can buy.
- *Brick and mortar.* If you don't have a good place to stash a body, build one!
- *Luminal.* Give yourself a chance to see where you missed cleaning up blood and other bodily fluids before the cops take a crack at it.
- *DVDs.* Do your research and buy up all the top crime TV shows, including all the *CSI*s, *Forensic File*s, and anything else you can get your hands on. You'll get an education you won't regret.

Friends in High—and Low—Places

As a mobster, you're going to make a lot of "friends" with local businessmen, and this will really come in handy for you when you need to get rid of a body. Make friends with the baker, and maybe he can be persuaded to grind bones into flour. The guy who owns the scrap yard can squash a corpse-filled car into a tuna can. You get the idea.

One of the best friends you'll ever make in the neighborhood is your local mortician. Not only can he cremate on command, he might also have a couple of double-body caskets on hand—which offer a secret lower compartment that can dispose of your victim at someone else's funeral. Talk about no fuss, no muss.

We'll get more into how to win over important friends and use their influence to your advantage in the next chapter.

Take It from Me . . .
Although it's impossible to recommend any particular body disposal method with 100 percent certainty, cremation is a popular, efficient alternative to the messy and time-consuming task of hacking a corpse into pieces. And let's face it: isn't it a whole lot easier to transport an urn of ashes then a batch of blood-soaked Hefty bags?

Closing Thoughts

Yes, it's true that violence will be like breathing for you from the minute you decide to embark on your Mafia career. It is, after all, how you control your universe. But that doesn't mean you can get cocky or lazy or too comfortable with it. You must be responsible and conscientious when it comes to committing—or ordering someone else to commit—acts of violence.

Random acts of violence are not encouraged and will ultimately lead to your demise. Sure, they happen all the time in Gangland. So does getting whacked. That doesn't mean you need to jump off that bridge. Just keep this as your mantra, and all will be well—until it isn't: Any day above ground is a good one.

And remember: No matter how good you are, there's always a chance you are going to get caught. But you want this chance to be in the smallest percentile imaginable. About as low as getting caught not paying your taxes. Or shot in the head while standing at a urinal.

CHAPTER 8

Handling the Law

or,

How to Make and Keep Friends in High Places

MICHAEL CORLEONE (Al Pacino): My father is no
  different than any powerful man, any man with
  power, like a president or senator.
KAY ADAMS (Diane Keaton): Do you know how naive
  you sound, Michael? Presidents and senators don't
  have men killed.
MICHAEL CORLEONE: Oh. Who's being naive, Kay?
  —*The Godfather* (1971)

ONCE YOU GET YOUR BUSINESS OFF THE GROUND, YOU'LL LIKELY NEED
to take great pains to keep it thriving. As head of your own
crime family, getting things going and keeping them going with
acts of violence both small and grandiose is only part of the
equation.

While you may not encounter any direct competition in your
neighborhood—that is, another Mafia family trying to hone in
on your territory—there are still many forces ready, eager, and
willing to trip you up, like cops, politicians, the feds. And despite how distracted they appear to be with all the terrorism

going on in the world right now, you can still bet that no one has a hard-on for you like the FBI.

So how do you stay at the top of your game and keep your enterprise thriving? This is the biggest challenge for any businessman but, of course, the legitimate businessman doesn't have the same troubles as you. And it's pretty likely his pockets are not as deep.

Yes, generosity, and lots of it, is the key here. To keep all those rackets of yours up and running, you're going to have to put some of that not-so-hard-earned cash to work. You're going to have to buy City Hall. Soon enough, you won't have room in your pockets for a gun anymore, they'll be too full of assembly leaders, committee members, judges, and police chiefs.

If you really play your cards right, you'll be rubbing shoulders with some of the most respectable folks in town—both because they're on the payroll and patronizing your brothels, gambling establishments, and dope dens. Just be prepared: They can also turn on you on a dime.

In this chapter, you will learn:

- How to encourage people in high places to help keep you in business—and out of trouble

- How to hire the right mob attorney

- What to do if you find yourself suddenly out of favors

Wiseguys in the Mainstream

The character Moe Greene in *The Godfather* was based on Bugsy Siegel.

First, the Voice in Your Head

Right now you're riding high, wide and handsome in big-shot gangster style, swaggering through life. But sometimes you get nagged by a still, small voice that says, *I love my life and how great everything's turned out . . . but isn't all this Mafia stuff maybe a bit, well, wrong and illegal?*

Your first target of influence is yourself and your conscience. If after all you've been through and built up at this point, that little whiny bitch—namely, your conscience—is still nagging you, put a hit on it—and quick. It's very bad for business.

Of course how you're conducting your life could be considered "wrong," but look at all the nice stuff you have now. And as far as it being "illegal"—well, nothing's illegal if you don't get caught.

You have to believe, without a fraction of doubt, in what you're doing here. It's the only way you're going to be able to convince important people they should be friends with you—that, and the money you give them. Remember: No one else is going to be buying into your brand of bullshit if you don't convincingly buy into it yourself, so the only thing that should be worrying that little brain of yours is getting caught. And even then, there are always options.

Making Friends with Other Influential People

Unfortunately, the days of simply handing off a weekly envelope to encourage do-gooders to look the other way are behind us. Nowadays, you need to be more clever with how the funds are funneled. While it's bad form nowadays to either give or receive bribes, there's absolutely nothing wrong with making a strategic—legitimately tax deductible!—campaign contribution or giant donation to the PBA (Police Benevolent Association). As with anything else you do in this business of yours, it's all about using your head.

If you're like most people, it's possible you've never had much use for politicians. Really, who has—what with their loose sets of morals, watered-down conviction, and slanting issues to suit their own political advancement? Now you do. Who better for a mobster to do business with than someone with loose morals, little or no conviction, and who will do anything to advance politically?

And now we're back to networking again. If a local politician knows you have a lot of pull with his or her constituency, that is, that you dominate and intimidate and essentially control how they make their decisions, that loose-moraled, convictionless, ambition whore is going to do whatever he or she can to make you happy.

Take It from Me . . .

Getting a politician in your pocket is like training a boxer or a race horse. It takes time and money, grooming, and preparing for the big payoff. And the more entries, the better your chances of winning.

A Beautiful Friendship

How you deal with cops will be a little different than with your friends in public office. Your relationship with the cops is more intimate; they're the ones who physically yearn to cuff you and drag you into the station, or shoot you dead in an alleyway. It's a very tactile relationship.

But it's also a symbiotic one. The cops are the yang to your yin and, without each other, neither could exist. You keep each other in balance. Each feeds the other one's needs. And that goes for local law enforcement and all the way up to the feds.

Many mobsters will tell you about their hatred for cops, and cops will tell you that mobsters are the scourge of the earth. But really, what fun would crime be without the element of danger—of getting caught? The thrill would be gone. And what would cops do all day without having someone to hunt and chase?

Every law enforcement agent and agency will tell you how society needs to rid itself of "that vile group called mobsters." But if their perfect world ever came to be, they'd all be jobless. Remember: Symbiotic.

If that little voice of yours still hasn't been snuffed out, maybe this will help: The Mafia is a public disservice that actually works to the service of the public. Think of all the guys who would be out of work if not for having to protect the streets and citizens from the likes of you. There's an unwanted dependency between the two groups, but it's there all the same.

Cops versus Mobsters: Mortal Enemies or One and the Same?

There have been many great cops who would have made excellent mobsters, and many legendary mobsters who would have made exceptional cops. Why is that? Well, when you get right down to it, there really isn't that much difference between the two groups—except which side of the line they walk. Both groups have a lot in common—more than either would ever admit. When a mobster looks in the mirror, on the other side is a cop, and vice versa. And don't we always hate in others what we see in ourselves?

Let's look at some of the similarities:

(continued on next page)

- Mobsters have the unwritten code of Omertà; cops have the unwritten code of ethics called "The Blue Wall."
- Both have a passion for perks, and enjoy free meals and other treats generously provided by neighborhood establishments craving protection.
- Both thrive on danger.
- Both are strong in their convictions. Whether you're a cop or a mobster, you're constantly putting your life on the line for what you believe, and will take all the necessary risks, be it to life or limb, to uphold these beliefs.
- Both have strong family values.
- Both feel the means justify the ends, and they'll use whatever means are necessary to get what they want—not letting truth or reality get in the way.
- Both can be bullies.
- Both believe that loyalty is everything.
- Both are committed for life.

Suddenly Scrupled

If you get caught, and the people you thought were your friends (because God knows you paid them enough to be) turn their backs on you, don't panic. It happens to everyone eventually. Remember to stay cool and keep the fact that an indictment is a long way off from a conviction running as a mantra in your mind.

If you get the right lawyer, you'll guarantee yourself a nice long, exhausting trial that will likely wear out anyone who wants to see you rot in the slammer, and you'll see that lots of opportunities to rectify the situation will present themselves as witnesses, jury members, and prosecuting attorneys will begin to feel worn down.

And for those who refuse to give up their pesky convictions, well, let's just say that if bribery or intimidation don't work, there's always your magical ability, with the help of your associates and underlings, of course, to make these "problems" disappear.

Lawyering Up

If all your efforts to stay off the police radar fail, you'll need to seek the assistance of a group whose avarice and viciousness makes the Mafia look tame: attorneys. And your understanding of why they're called "criminal lawyers" will be complete upon receipt of their bill for services rendered.

The important thing here is that no matter how panicked you feel about the situation, take your time in choosing the best attorney you can find. Do an Internet search of mob trials throughout the years. Find out who defended whom—as well as who was successful in getting his client off, and who was an abysmal failure. Lay as much groundwork as possible before hiring any lawyer, and you'll leave little room for later surprises.

Here are some qualities you'll want to look for in a mob lawyer:

- *A strong sense of self.* It takes balls to stand up in court and lie through one's teeth about how valuable a member of society you are—even if he knows the exact number of widows you've created.

- *A proven track record.* How will you know if he's worth the payout if you haven't seen what he can do? Ask a lot of questions. Ask to see trial videos of him defending other mobsters, if he has them. It's your life we're talking about here—impose all you want.

- *A designer wardrobe and impressive watch.* This goes along with the track record thing. If he's successful, he should flaunt it—just as you do.

- *No moral core.* If he lacks the ability to sleep at night after putting the likes of you back on the streets, he's not the right fit.

- *A complete disregard for humanity.* Why else would he or she even consider protecting the rights of a monster like you?

Whatever you do, avoid getting saddled with a public defender at all costs—even if it costs you nothing. These guys may seem like they're working for you, but they're part of the system. You get what you pay for. Pay nothing, and you should expect nothing in return. Pay handsomely, and you should expect a handsome reward in the form of your freedom. And if your pricey lawyer is not able to get you off, feel free to sick your goons on him to break one of his bones for every dollar he stole from you.

Doing Time

So many of the greats in Mafia history, whether the real deal or on the big or small screen, have had to do time at some point or other. Sometimes the busts have been big, sometimes it's bullshit, but it still means an interruption in the lifestyle you worked so hard to create for yourself. But it doesn't have to mean going out of business.

As this could become your reality at some point, it is advised that you take precautions to ensure your business will keep running should you ever find yourself in the slammer. Make sure your underboss and consigliere are apprised of the details of your business. Instruct your capos to inflict as much damage as possible on the stoolie that turned you in or the cop that arrested you—and/or their families. Just note: It's preferable that those who turned against you be forced to live and suffer the consequences than be granted peace and ignorance in death.

While you're locked away, try and make the most of your free time. Plot revenge. Read up on criminal law loopholes. Strategize the future of your business. Eventually, they're gonna let you out, so you might as well be ready to tackle the world again when you're sprung.

Talk the Talk, Part 5

Hack: Another name for a prison guard—a guy who essentially couldn't cut it as a cop, or even a mall security guard.

Heat: You want to avoid heat (unwanted attention from the law or the press) at all costs. Unless you flee to Tahiti. In which case, you want as much heat as possible.

On the pad: The only way to stay "off the short list" of law enforcement is to stay "on the pad"—in other words, keep their pockets full and their bank account balances flourishing.

Pinched: One of the worst fates you can expect as a mobster. "Getting pinched" means getting arrested.

Uncle Sugar: Kind of a smart ass way to refer to the feds.

Closing Thoughts

Getting caught isn't fun. Whether or not you have to serve time, the costs can very well put you out of business. That's why it's essential to keep your trap shut, cover your tracks, and be as "generous" as you can with anyone who can help you stay out of harm's way. As with everything, there are exceptions, but if you keep watching your ass, the chances that you'll get pinched will decrease significantly.

CHAPTER 9

Welcome to the Big Time!

or,

You're Only as Good as Your Getaway Plan

MICHAEL CORLEONE (Al Pacino): I feel . . . I'm getting
  wiser now.
KAY CORLEONE (Diane Keaton): The sicker you get, the
  wiser you get, huh?
MICHAEL CORLEONE: When I'm dead, I'm gonna be
  really smart.
  —*The Godfather Part III* (1990)

YOU'VE FOLLOWED ALL THE INSTRUCTIONS IN THIS BOOK AND YOU'RE
finally ready to sit back and enjoy your success. You are feared,
loved, and respected by business owners, law makers, and friends
and family members. You've got so much tax-free income, you
have no idea where to spend it. You have a designer wardrobe,
a collection of gold watches and chains you've received on the
brooch, and a goomar for every night of the week.

Now what?

It's time to safeguard your empire from anyone wishing to infiltrate it, as essentially just keep yourself alive and out of the clink for as long as you possibly can.

Wiseguys in the Mainstream

The novel *Billy Bathgate* (1989) is about Dutch Schultz's last days. (Dustin Hoffman plays Schultz in the movie version.)

Staying Viable in Today's Competitive Crime Environment

Making the big time is no time to start getting lazy. Once others see the success you've made of yourself tapping previously untapped markets and generating wads of cash, you should expect there to be some kind of following.

Nip it in the bud. You're not in the business of being a mentor to any aspiring mobsters and you don't need to inspire others to try and take over all you've been able to build up. If others in your neighborhood start forming families of their own, wipe them out—and quickly.

You are the neighborhood fear-monger; you, and your family, are the only ones in your vicinity who should be dealing in organized crime. Even if you don't live past next Tuesday, you have your wife and kids to consider. You may not be immortal, but you should think of your business running forever.

What Can You Expect Now?

As you enter the golden era of your crime career, there are four basic realities for you. It's almost definite that one of these will become your fate:

- Death by getting whacked by someone in another family—or even someone in your own family

- Death by the legal system. This could mean a quiet execution via electric chair or lethal injection—or a fiery blaze in an alleyway by a band of trigger-happy G-men

- Life in prison—which may as well be death

- Witness protection program. But we'll talk about this later.

Don't expect to die of natural causes when you're ninety. Live as though you will be dead tomorrow. That means enjoying every minute of your evil empire, but also making sure your family is provided for.

When You're Gone

In the perfect scenario, your infrastructure will be strong enough to run itself without you—and that means forever, if you get yourself whacked—or even temporarily, if you happen to get pinched.

In the second scenario, keep in mind that family loyalties will be tested and determined by the length of your sentence. If you're away one to five years, your people will probably stick around—especially if you can keep things running from your cell, and because there's a chance you'll be out soon enough to bash in skulls should any of your people be disloyal. If you're in for life, you better hope you generated enough fear in your people to last their lifetime. Otherwise, it's all going to fall apart.

The most important thing that must be stressed here is that you need to have an understanding of the eventual obsolescence of your position—and a Plan A, Plan B, Plan C, even Plan D for what comes next. Whether you're arrested, rubbed out, or somehow disappear, you're only as good as your getaway plan.

Wiseguys in the Mainstream

Dick Tracy's Alphonse "Big Boy" Caprice is based on Al Capone—ironic because in the film version of the comic strip, this character is played by Al Pacino, who starred in the 1983 version of *Scarface*, a film based on the life of Al Capone.

A Word About Stoolies and the Witness Protection Program

If you're in it, you're a rat. And we don't like your kind. Rats need to be exterminated; we will find you. If you've gotten yourself in so deep that you need to break Omertà and blab on your Italian brothers, you're probably better off just offing yourself. No mortician, no matter how skilled or experienced or qualified, will be able to guarantee an open casket once we get through with you.

Take It from Me...

Now is the time to make sure eyes have developed in the back of your head. It's also the time to make plans for your demise, because demise is inevitable.

Closing Thoughts

When all is said and done, a mobster's life is not an easy one. Sure, you're not going to get perks like these anywhere else. And yes, there's the women. But just like all good things, it will eventually come to an end.

If you're lucky, you'll get to wrap your career in legendary style. You won't be forced into early retirement and given a token watch for thirty-or-so years of indentured servitude; you'll get yours right on the front lines, in the line of duty. And if you get whacked, you'll not only enjoy a place in Mafia folklore, you won't have to rot away the rest of your life in a jail cell, where the closest thing to prosciutto you'll ever get is baloney on white. That's no life for you.

A bullet to the back of your brain as you savor a bowl of pasta is the best possible ending you can hope for in your mobster career. If you can help it, just try and get yourself killed after or, at the very least, during your meal; it's a total disgrace for a mobster to die on an empty stomach.